Adventures in singlehood

Adventures in singlehood

A ROAD MAP FOR SINGLES

**SUSIE SHELLENBERGER
& MICHAEL ROSS**

ZondervanPublishingHouse
Grand Rapids, Michigan

A Division of HarperCollins*Publishers*

Adventures in Singlehood
Copyright © 1996 by Susie Shellenberger and Michael Ross

Requests for information should be addressed to:

ZondervanPublishingHouse
Grand Rapids, Michigan 49530

Library of Congress Cataloging-in-Publication Data

Shellenberger, Susie.
    Adventures in singlehood : a road map for singles / Susie Shellenberger and
Michael Ross.
      p.   cm.
    ISBN: 0-310-20177-2
    1. Single people—Religious life. 2. Single people—Conduct of life. I. Ross,
Michael, 1961– . II. Title.
BV4596.S5S48   1996
248.8'4—dc20   95-42333
                                                        CIP

We gratefully acknowledge permission to reprint the song "Great Is Thy
Faithfulness." Words: Thomas O. Chisholm, 1923. Music: William M. Runyan, 1923.
Copyright 1923. Renewal 1951 by Hope Publishing Co., Carol Stream, IL 60188. All
rights reserved. Used with permission.

"Top 10 Things Not to Say to a Single" by Susan Maycinik first appeared in the
May/June 1994 *Discipleship Journal* and is reprinted with permission.

"Sex Under Control" by Archibald Hart first appeared in the November/December
1994 issue of *New Man* magazine and is used with permission.

"The Secret of Love" excerpted with permission from *Tell Me the Secrets*, by Max
Lucado. Crossway Books, 1993. All rights reserved.

All Scripture quotations, unless otherwise indicated, are taken from the *Holy Bible:
New International Version®*. NIV®. Copyright © 1973, 1978, 1984 by International
Bible Society. Used by permission of Zondervan Publishing House. All rights
reserved.

Published in association with the literary agency of Alive Communications, Inc., 1465
Kelly Johnson Blvd., Suite 320, Colorado Springs, CO 80920

Edited by Rachel Boers
Interior design by Sherri L. Hoffman
Interior illustrations by Barb Hranilovich

Printed in the United States of America

95 96 97 98 99 00 01 02 /❖ DH/ 10 9 8 7 6 5 4 3 2 1

To
Dr. and Mrs. Woodie J. Stevens
who loved me into being whole when
I felt extremely new and alone

To
Tiffany Cox—my favorite West Virginian:
"God is love. Whoever lives in love
lives in God, and God in him."

Contents

A ROAD MAP

Congratulations! You've started this book at the same place a million other singles have. (Okay . . . maybe not a *million,* but at least thirty—all our friends and relatives promised they'd buy and read it.)

Now the rest is up to you. That's right. You don't have to start with the first chapter, because you may not need it. You might, however, need something from the middle or toward the back. *You* decide where you want to go next.

Just so you won't get lost on this adventure, we've provided a map to follow at your own pace and direction.

➤ "I'm tired of being single . . . and I'm tired of waiting for that special someone." Skip over to "Why Am I Still Single?" on page 15.

➤ "I want to discover ways of being more fulfilled as a single." Start this book with "Filling the Void of Loneliness" on page 31.

➤ "I'm thirsty for ideas on how my church can do a better job of meeting the needs of singles." Fill your gas tank at "What Churches Can Do to Include Singles" on page 45.

➡ "I'd like to develop more friendships with the opposite sex." Skip to "Sparking Friendships With the Opposite Sex" on page 59.

➡ "I'm tired of traveling solo. I'd like to share my lifetime adventure. What steps should I take to attract a mate ... and where should I look?" Slam your brakes when you get to "Attracting a Mate Without Being Obvious" on page 67.

➡ "Where can I meet someone who would make a good date?" Cruise over to "How to Meet Potential Dates" on page 75.

➡ "My current relationship is way too physical." Check out "Creating Safeguards" on page 83.

➡ "I've had my heart stepped on too many times. What am I doing wrong?" Take a look at "Brokenhearted: How to Survive Breakups" on page 93.

➡ "I'm in a relationship right now ... but I wish I weren't. Breaking up is definitely in our future, but I'm not sure how to do it." Head over to "Breaking Hearts: How to Break Up Without a Black Eye" on page 99.

➡ "I really *try* to understand the opposite sex, but we just seem so different. I'm frustrated." Don't miss "Basic Major Differences Between Men and Women" on page 105.

➡ "I'd like to tap into a woman's head and pull out some of her thoughts. Maybe then I could figure out how to understand her." Flip to "She Said That, but He Heard This" on page 113.

➤ "I want to learn what personality type is most compatible with me." Take a shortcut to "Keys to Understanding" on page 119.

➤ "I want to do all I can right now to become everything my future partner needs me to be." Catch a glimpse of "Becoming the Mate Your Future Spouse Will Need" on page 131.

➤ "Women face pressures men can't begin to understand. How can guys learn more about us?" Route them over to "From the Heart of a Woman" on page 143.

➤ "What are the roadblocks to true manhood?" Meet us at "From the Heart of a Man" on page 149.

➤ "I'm thirty years old, single, and starting to panic! Can you even come *close* to understanding what I'm feeling?" Turn to "A Compass That Comforts" on page 159.

➤ "I imagine when I find true love, it's going to feel pretty good. *Isn't* it?" Follow your road map to "In the Arms of Love Without Getting Strangled" on page 165.

➤ "I've established a steady trail of romantic love, but I want *more*. I'm looking for a 'cap' on this whole adventure." Journey over to "One Last Thing About Love" on page 177.

PART ONE:

Dealing With Singleness

CHAPTER 1

Why Am I Still Single?

I ask this nagging question every April 5th—my birthday. Each year on this date, I blow out one more candle and sit through yet another "It's-time-we-get-you-married" lecture from well-meaning church friends. And each year I ask, Is this the year I'm going to get married?

Twelve months later I find myself in the same predicament: alone.

I'm never more reminded of my marital status, or lack of it, than when I see a public display of affection: a lip-locked couple blocking access to the mall's only ATM machine; newlyweds playfully feeding each other popcorn at the movie theater; new parents beaming with pride as their "terrible twos" toddler takes his first ride on the electric pony. Each time I'm confronted with one of these situations, the question wells up inside: *Lord, why am I still single?*

A while back, my sister Barbara and I took a thirty-minute train trip from downtown Boston to her home in Wakefield. By the way, Barbara's happily married, with a daughter, two dogs, and a cat.

We'd just ended a busy day of shopping and were thoroughly worn out. As the crowded train began to rumble down the tracks, a young man squeezed into a seat in front of us. Tucked under one arm was a bag with a large bow on a brightly wrapped gift peeking out. He wrestled off his jacket and carefully situated the package on his lap. Then he leaned against the window and rested his arm on the back of the seat.

I noticed a wedding ring on his hand. Suddenly, I felt old. I mean, this guy looked like he was fresh out of high school . . . and married?! What's more, during the entire train ride, he was constantly looking down at the package, adjusting the bow, and smiling from ear to ear. He seemed to radiate joy.

Once again, I was instantly reminded of my singleness. *I bet the gift is for his wife,* I thought. *It must be a romantic occasion. She must be terrific. He has someone special in his life. Lucky guy.*

A few rows ahead, I spotted a couple sitting especially close and staring into each other's eyes. Occasionally, she'd stroke his hair and giggle, and he'd return with a gentle peck on her cheek.

I sighed and glanced at my sister, who smiled and looked out the window. I'm sure she had no idea of the hollow ache in my heart.

Have I missed the train? Will I ever share my life with someone special? Will I ever be married? Lord, why am I still single?

———— ⋄ ————

For Mike, seeing a happy young man wearing a wedding ring and toting a beautiful package triggered something that is familiar to all singles: aloneness.

I was overwhelmed with aloneness just a few weeks ago. The scene? Church. I had just finished teaching an adult Sunday school class. It had gone great. Most of our regulars were there, and we even had quite a few visitors. So I should have been feeling secure, fulfilled, needed.

Instead, after class I walked into the sanctuary to sit with friends. From my vantage point, I couldn't help but see my friend Kerry slip his arm around his wife, Kim. As he did so, she leaned a little closer into his shoulder. And even though I was listening to the sermon, I couldn't help thinking, *Kerry and Kim really belong together.*

My gaze wandered toward the front of the sanctuary, where I observed Jeff and Kathy. *What a neat team they make,* I thought. *They're both involved in the music program; they love people. They even look good together. It's obvious Jeff and Kathy belong together.*

As the congregation stood, I noticed Brian and Diane, Tom and Shelly, Tim and Cindy. *Each belongs to the other,* I thought. Watching Tim slip his arm around the waist of his wife, I caught myself thinking, *I want someone to put his arm around my waist.* My friends Shirley and Greg—who were sitting next to me—were sharing their hymnal. *I would love to share a hymnal,* I mused. *It's so obvious. Everyone belongs to someone. But who do I belong to?*

And my aloneness hit me.

Hard.

Please understand. I wasn't feeling sorry for myself. I can, however, throw a pretty mean pity party! I simply wanted to belong. To be included. To be a part of someone. To have someone think I am special enough to put an arm around my waist. To know someone's unconditional, no-strings-attached love. *I'm tired, God,* I prayed silently. *Tired of being strong. Tired of walking into church alone. Tired of wondering what it would feel like to spend the rest of my life with a man who is my absolute very best friend in the world. Will I ever be married? Lord, why am I still single?*

ALONENESS TRIGGERS

God desires each one of us to live victoriously. We can't help being affected by our circumstances to some degree, but when we allow our reactions and emotions to be controlled by what's going on around us, we're distancing ourselves from God's best for us.

We all have certain things that trigger or make us more aware of our singleness. It only makes sense, then, to either stay away from these triggers or, if they're unavoidable, to mentally prepare ourselves for them in advance.

Most singles wrestle with insecurities, doubts, loneliness, and that nagging question: Lord, why am I still single? Hopefully, though, you don't battle these issues every day, because if you do, you're probably living a miserable life. The truth is that even though most of us who are single would really like to be married, there is no reason why we cannot be whole, fulfilled, full of peace, and fun to be around just as we are!

There are, however, certain things or situations or times of the year that trigger the *aloneness factor*.

Here Comes the Bride

I realized recently that weddings are sometimes a trigger for me. Shannon was a member of my Sunday school class who had invited me to her big day. I not only wanted to go, but as her teacher, I also felt a responsibility to attend. I knew, however, that I didn't want to go alone, so I rode to the ceremony with Diane—another friend from the class.

The church was packed and the stage elegantly decorated with greenery and elaborate candelabra. I watched the groomsmen and the bridesmaids take their places with a wave of emotion sweeping over me.

And then I saw Shannon. She looked so beautiful as she walked down the aisle to join her soon-to-be husband. I fought back the tears. As the ceremony continued and they exchanged vows, I couldn't help but think, *Lord, will that ever be me? Will I walk down the aisle someday to be greeted by my best friend/lover/soul mate?*

The bride and groom took Communion together. The music was fabulous. The audience smiled their approval. But I continued my one-sided conversation. *What is it? Am I not good enough? Have I been too career-minded?*

I skipped the reception and went home, extremely aware of my singlehood, my aloneness. Before throwing myself into a book project I was working on, I took the time to make a long-distance phone call to a close friend, Susan.

We laughed, talked about my friend's softball team, laughed, talked about my writing project, and laughed some more. When I was ready to hang up, Susan said, "Susie, what can I do for you?"

I denied that I needed anything and told her I had simply called to shoot the breeze. She paused, then repeated the question, "Susie, what can I do for you?" Again, I laughed and made small talk and tried to hang up. But she wouldn't let it die. Once more, "What can I do for you?" And I began to cry. "I think I just need a hug," I said.

My Wife Always Says . . .

Another common situation that can trigger aloneness is when we're with a group of married people who consistently talk about their spouses. Though they certainly don't mean to exclude anyone, they automatically do alienate those who are single by continuing conversations centered around things that only couples enjoy or talk about.

I went to Uganda, Africa, last year with a small group of people. We were there a little over a week, and we had come from a variety of sources for one reason: to report on AIDS for our particular newspaper or magazine. As you can imagine, it was an extremely powerful trip that was difficult, even heart-breaking, at times.

When we'd gather for dinner in the evening, our group would talk through the events of the day. And, probably as a tension reliever from the sadness we'd faced just hours before, members of the group would inevitably start sharing about their spouses, home, and kids.

Even though I realized the group members longed for their loved ones, I couldn't help feeling excluded. Having everyone talk about their families triggered a sense of aloneness within me. I was suddenly acutely aware of my singleness.

What can you do when you find yourself in a similar situation? One of the things I found helpful was to talk about what is dear to my heart. While others bragged about their kids, I talked about my dog. When others would look at pictures of their spouses, I'd laugh and pull out my golden retriever's photo to pass it around. Even though I felt alone on the inside, I determined to fit in with my surroundings on the outside.

I also discovered it helps to focus on the lives of others. To divert my attention from how alone and excluded I felt, I began involving myself in others' stories. I asked questions about their spouses, their home lives, their children. People love to talk about themselves and their families. When feeling lonely, why not immerse yourself into getting to know someone else a little better?

If I Were Married . . .

Another common trigger is to feel aloneness when faced with a specific problem that seems overwhelming. The problem may actually be small but perception tends to determine reality. For me, car problems are frustrating. When I needed to attach license plates to my car, I remember thinking, *If I were married, I wouldn't have to worry about this.* I ended up waiting until my parents came to visit and asked Dad to put them on for me!

And then, about a month before Thanksgiving, a friend and I were driving from Colorado Springs to Denver for a concert. As we headed toward the interstate, she said, "Susie, what's that noise your car is making?"

"What noise?" I asked.

"Listen."

"I don't hear anything."

"Something's wrong," she insisted. We pulled over, and she got out and looked at my tires. "There's a huge screw in your rear tire!" she exclaimed.

I got out of the car, squatted down, and strained my eyes. Sure enough—there it was, big as day, a big old screw sticking out of my tire.

"Well, it's not leaking air," I reasoned. "Let's just forget about it and go on to Denver."

After that, I prayed daily that my tire would be okay until my parents arrived for Thanksgiving. *Dad'll fix it,* I reasoned, but I couldn't help but think how much easier life would be if I had a husband to change and fix my tire.

Maybe you are frustrated when you try to disconnect the sprinkler system for the winter, or kill a spider, or determine if there's a mouse in the house. All these things are responsibilities I would love to pass on to a husband. Whatever the source of frustration, being forced to deal with it by yourself can be a trigger to feeling alone.

Be Willing to Ask for Help

Everyone wants to feel needed. I used to think asking for help was a sign of weakness. I'm learning, though, that people usually enjoy being needed, and most of the time when I solicit help, the person I seek out is usually more than willing to offer services. When I allow another person to meet some of my needs, it gives someone else a chance to minister.

So when I needed to buy and plant a tree, I asked Tim if he could help. He not only helped, he borrowed a truck to haul the tree in, brought two shovels and a package of shrub

A number of situations trigger aloneness in men, too. I (Mike) met a guy named Curtis at a singles' retreat at which he was speaking in Colorado. During a small group session, Curtis poured out his heart about a situation that had caused him to feel alone. Here's his story:

It was the worst day of my life. The night before, I went to bed lonely . . . and woke up with my heart still aching and my head pounding. Even my dreams were grim! To top it off, it was Monday and my alarm clock didn't go off, so I was late for work.

I rushed around my apartment, looking for the only tie that goes with my brown jacket, while at the same time brushing my teeth and running a comb through that matted mop on my head.

Lord, what's the point? I silently cried out. *I'm so lonely! My family lives miles from me. I'm new here and don't have too many real friends. And I come home each night to an empty place. If it weren't for Bart (my cat) I'd go crazy.*

By the way, I thought to myself, *where is Bart? Usually he's mauling me for a meal at about this time.*

After spitting and rinsing, I grabbed my keys and headed for the car.

"You lose, Bart," I mumbled. "Guess you'll have to catch a mouse for breakfast!"

I pulled away from the curb, only to slam on the brakes two seconds later. "No way!" I yelled. "It can't be. Lord, please don't let that tiny, curled-up ball of fur be Bart!"

I hopped out of my car and raced to the side of the road. I had always feared this would happen one day.

The street I live on is very busy, and Bart always insisted upon crossing it to check out the action in my neighbor's yard.

My furry friend—my only pal in this town—lay lifeless on the ground.

I cradled Bart in my arms and wept. *Lord, my life feels like one big empty mess. I'm alone. And now I don't even have Bart. What's the point, Lord?*

God helped me through that hard point in my life. He showed me there is a great point to my life . . . in spite of being single. He also gave me this message: "Be still, Curtis. Be still and know that I am God. Wait upon me, and trust that I will fulfill the desires of your heart. I will provide for your needs."

Sometimes being single is hard. Most of us yearn for someone in the flesh whom we can spend our lives with. Waiting isn't easy. But with Jesus in your heart, you already have the ultimate relationship. And, trust me, he will soothe the ache if you just let him.

vitamins, and planted it for me. And when my car broke down, Cheryl not only drove through a snowstorm to get me, but also loaned me her car for a week.

In times of frustration and problems, it's probably natural to think, *If only I were married . . . my husband would take care of this.* Or, *This is something my wife would be really good at.* Instead of concentrating on your aloneness, allow someone else to minister to you to meet your needs.

Just Me and This Motel Room

Since I'm usually speaking somewhere within the United States about every other weekend, I travel a lot. Most singles who travel know how being on the road can often make us keenly aware of our aloneness. Married friends carry photos of their families, call their spouses when they arrive at their destination, and are able to rest in the assurance that someone's missing them while they're away.

To combat feelings of aloneness when you're traveling, try talking to the One who is always with you. When you're feeling alone and uncared for, concentrate on giving those feelings to your heavenly Father. He's in that motel room with you, sharing your feelings, hearing your thoughts, and seeing your hurt. Take advantage of the aloneness you feel by soaking up some special promises from the Word or lifting others and their needs in prayer.

And don't forget this handy tip: Reach out and touch someone. Okay, so you're not married. Obviously, you can't call your husband or wife, but make plans ahead of time to call a close friend. I call someone every time I'm out of town.

I also take pictures of my family (parents, my brother's family, my pastor's family, my dog, my college roommate and her family, etc.) with me. Not a trip goes by that I don't open my ticket pouch, pull out those photos, and look at each one.

So Don't Go!

Of course, you can always avoid some events that serve as natural triggers to your aloneness. The hard part is deciding which is worse: missing the event, or how you'll feel while attending the event.

PLAN AHEAD

Whether it be an office party, a baby or wedding shower, or a small group activity, you can learn to deal effectively with your aloneness and live a fulfilled life in spite of being a single in a couples' world.

If you know a specific situation will trigger your aloneness and you can't avoid it, at least make active plans to help curb the trigger.

Looking back to the wedding incident at the beginning of the chapter, I hadn't attended a wedding in a few years, and they had never triggered my aloneness before. But now I was a few years older. Even though I couldn't verbalize what I was feeling before I left, I suspected I'd need a friend. That's why I called Diane and asked if we could attend together.

Enlist the help of friends. Though I didn't share with Diane what I was feeling, just being with another person provided a bit of comfort during a ceremony that celebrated couplehood.

Be honest with friends. Once I decided to tell Susan what was really bothering me, I realized simply verbalizing the problem helped.

Look at both sides. Susan listened to me as I shared how lonely I felt and reiterated my desire to be married. When I was ready to listen, she told about the opposite side. It helped to be reminded by this married friend of mine of all the advantages I have simply because I'm single. I can pick up and leave whenever I want. I'm independent. I can spend the money I make on me and not have to worry about children's dentist bills or what my husband would think about each purchase I make.

After talking about the positive side to singlehood, I hung up the phone and smiled. *I really have it pretty good,* I thought. *If God wants me married, he's certainly big enough to bring just the right man into my life at just the right time.*

PROS AND CONS

There are advantages to being single—as well as a few disadvantages. Maybe you can add your own thoughts to the following lists. Then, whenever the blues hit, read through the following pros and cons and smile until you laugh.

Advantages of Being Single

- Toss the dirty dishes and laundry in the tub with you when you take a bath. No sense wasting water, right? Just clean it all at once!
- Why change the sheets? After a couple of years, they'll actually disintegrate.
- Really tired? You can go to bed at 8 P.M. without feeling guilty.
- You can sing as loud as you want with the stereo—and pretend you're Amy Grant or Michael W. Smith, complete with dance moves and curtain calls.
- You can eat cereal for breakfast, lunch, and dinner, and no one cares.
- You can eat chocolate for breakfast, lunch, and dinner, and no one cares.
- You don't have to decorate for Christmas if you don't want to.
- You can get by with just bringing a bag of rolls instead of a roast for church potlucks.
- It doesn't matter how long you leave your smelly workout clothes in the backseat of your car.
- You can cry as much as you want without having to explain to someone what's wrong.

Disadvantages of Being Single

- There's no one to help you zip up the back of your dress.
- No one meets you at the airport when you return from an out-of-town trip.

- There's no one to share the blame for a messy house, and you have to clean everything yourself.
- It can sometimes take over a month just to have enough dishes to fill the dishwasher for a full wash cycle.
- You can cry all evening, but no one's going to ask you what's wrong or if you'd like to talk about it.
- The invitation to the company picnic always reads, "For you and your spouse."
- Most coupons say, "Buy one dinner, get one free." Great. What are you going to do with two dinners?

TRUE CONTENTMENT

One snowy Sunday morning, I was sitting in church in the front row with three friends. The church choir had already sung the special music. Announcements had been made. But just before our pastor stepped behind the pulpit to share God's Word with the congregation, we rose to our feet as the screen bearing the words to an old, old hymn spilled from the ceiling.

The organist began, and we lifted our voices. *Was everyone getting louder, or was it just the rhythm inside* me *that was swelling in praise?* I stopped for a moment to take in the harmony surrounding me, then continued with everyone else. "Great is Thy faithfulness! ... All I have needed Thy hand hath provided. ..."

My eyes filled with tears as I silently thanked the Lord for being such a powerful, dependable Father. *You really have provided, Lord,* I prayed. *That's the key, isn't it? Your promise to fulfill me. And if that's really true, then it doesn't matter if I'm single or if I'm married. You have promised to fill my life with yourself, your Spirit, your personality, your power!*

Isaiah 54:5 jumped into my mind: "Your Creator will be your 'husband'"(TLB). Even though I stood in a large church surrounded by others, it was as though God and I were alone—face-to-face, heart-to-heart—and he was speaking to me in an intimate way. "My promise," he was telling me, "is that I will take care of you forever. Don't be afraid. You're not alone. I will pour my vision into your mind. Dream big dreams—after all, you're serving a giant God. Do not allow your singleness to hold you back. I will give you everything you need to fulfill my plan for your life."

That's true contentment. And most of the time it's not something we just fall into; rather, it's something that has to be learned. It didn't come naturally to the apostle Paul to be content in any situation that existed; he worked hard to learn it. You have a choice: You can concentrate on your aloneness, or you can choose to believe that God dreams big dreams for all his children. I choose to think God has big dreams for me.

The great thing is that if we work at being content, our Father has promised to provide the assurance, the strength, and the comfort we need.

Here are the words to the song I sang in church the day I realized again how great God's faithfulness is to us. Go ahead. Sing them. No one's listening. Or, better yet, memorize them. That way you can sing them over and over and over again— at the precise moment you need them the most.

Great Is Thy Faithfulness

Great is Thy faithfulness, O God, my Father!
There is no shadow of turning with Thee;
Thou changest not—Thy compassions, they fail not:
As Thou hast been Thou forever wilt be.
Great is Thy faithfulness!
Great is Thy faithfulness!

Morning by morning new mercies I see;
All I have needed Thy hand hath provided—
Great is Thy faithfulness,
Lord, unto me!

Summer and winter and springtime and harvest,
Sun, moon and stars in their courses above,
Join with all nature in manifold witness
To Thy great faithfulness, mercy and love.
Great is Thy faithfulness!
Great is Thy faithfulness!
Morning by morning new mercies I see;
All I have needed Thy hand hath provided—
Great is Thy faithfulness,
Lord, unto me!

Pardon for sin and a peace that endureth,
Thine own dear presence to cheer and to guide,
Strength for today and bright hope for tomorrow—
Blessings all mine, with ten thousand beside!
Great is Thy faithfulness!
Great is Thy faithfulness!
Morning by morning new mercies I see;
All I have needed Thy hand hath provided.
Great is Thy faithfulness—
Lord unto me!

CHAPTER 2

Filling the Void of Loneliness

It's unrealistic and just plain stupid to think that another person can make us whole. Yet, I have numerous single friends who can't wait to be married. They're assuming a mate will fill that aching void of loneliness in their lives.

A mate will certainly enhance our lives . . . but fill the void? Is it fair to expect anyone to accomplish a task as big and important as that?

God's ideal is for us to be whole as individuals. Then when we marry, we marry already whole. Our mate simply adds to our life, instead of becoming our life. When we make God the center of our lives, he brings the fulfillment and security we need. Then when we marry, we do so as two whole people enhancing the lives of each other.

I've come to realize that Jesus Christ is the only One who can fill the void in my life. My security, happiness, and fulfillment have to be grounded in a relationship with him, not with another human.

Only when I'm whole in Christ will I be ready to join a lifetime commitment with someone else. I cannot go into a marriage expecting this person to make me whole. Too many insecure people come together expecting to gain wholeness from their spouse. The result? Two incomplete individuals.

Let's take a deeper look at loneliness.

EXPERIENCING LONELINESS

Loneliness is universal in our world. Psychologists tell us it's one of the most frequent issues they deal with in counseling. Loneliness is often the root of suicide attempts, drug abuse, addiction to alcohol, and many other problems, both physical and psychological.

Ironically, out of all the problems that surround us, loneliness is the most frequently mentioned problem in our society. Doctors tell us that loneliness is as significant to high blood pressure as obesity is to a lack of exercise. Medical experts also point out that loneliness—social isolation—is a greater mortality risk than smoking.

Someone once described loneliness as "sensing the spirit of one you love pulling away from you." Let's take a look at Matthew 26:36–46, 56 (TLB):

> Then Jesus brought them to a garden grove, Gethsemane, and told them to sit down and wait while He went on ahead to pray. He took Peter with him and Zebedee's two sons James and John, and began to be filled with anguish and despair.
>
> Then he told them, "My soul is crushed with horror and sadness to the point of death . . . stay here . . . stay awake with me."
>
> He went forward a little, and fell face downward on the ground, and prayed, "My Father! If it is possible, let this cup be taken away from me. But I want your will, not mine."
>
> Then he returned to the three disciples and found them asleep. "Peter," he called, "couldn't you even

stay awake with me one hour? Keep alert and pray. Otherwise temptation will overpower you. For the spirit indeed is willing, but how weak the body is!"

Again, he left them and prayed, "My Father! If this cup cannot go away until I drink it all, your will be done."

He returned to them again and found them sleeping, for their eyes were heavy, so he went back to prayer the third time, saying the same things again.

Then he came to the disciples and said, "Sleep on now and take your rest . . . but no! The time has come! I am betrayed into the hands of evil men! Up! Let's be going! Look! Here comes the man who is betraying me!"

At that point, all the disciples deserted him and fled.

What a powerful commentary on loneliness. It's described in these verses as "those we love forsaking us when we need them the most." When we're lonely, we're reminded how Jesus Christ feels when we drift away from him.

It's easy for us to imagine the emptiness we would feel if a loved one were to separate from us, but we can't begin to comprehend the loneliness God felt when man was eternally separated from him, the Father Creator. Out of love, he created a bridge. That bridge is his Son, Jesus.

He became our bridge so we will never be separated from our heavenly Father again. In other words, we need never be lonely.

As singles, we know all too well what loneliness feels like. And it doesn't feel good. No one enjoys sitting at home . . . alone . . . while friends are out on dates or while families create an atmosphere of warmth and fun in their homes.

Sometimes loneliness is caused by what we do ourselves. Other times, it is caused by circumstances beyond our control or society. Loneliness can be separated into several categories:

1. Loneliness caused by isolating ourselves. We become negative, sarcastic, and cynical. We complain, harbor a bitter spirit, and eventually drive others away.

You probably know someone like this. To be around him or her for any length of time is simply emotionally draining; he or she wears you out. What kind of person are you? Do you drain people? Are you always taking, asking advice, or criticizing the way things are done? Or are you willing to give, listen, share, smile, and radiate a positive, caring spirit?

2. Loneliness caused by circumstances beyond our control. This type of loneliness doesn't happen because you're a bad person or because you're difficult to be around. You don't cause this loneliness—God allows it, not out of anger or spite, but because we live in a fallen world. Sometimes bad things happen to good people. In other words, a loved one dies or best friends move away. This usually requires an adjustment period . . . requiring change . . . which is never easy.

I remember when my ninety-six-year-old grandmother died. She was a saint. She prayed for me every single day of my life. I can't tell you what a comfort it was to know that someone interceded to the Father daily on my behalf. Her death left a hole in my heart. That is one less person praying for me.

It was hard on our entire family . . . especially my mother. She and Grandmother talked on the phone every day. It was hard to believe the phone would never ring again with her voice on the other end.

If you're experiencing this kind of loneliness, let me encourage you to begin praying for healing. In Psalm 34, God promises to be very close to those whose hearts are breaking.

He's also promised to be our Comforter. He can begin the healing process right now if you'll trust him with the hurt. And it is a process. Sometimes wounds take a long time to heal.

3. *Loneliness caused by spiritual or psychological loneliness.* It's strange how we can be surrounded by crowds of people and yet still feel completely alone, isn't it? We've all heard the saying, "It's lonely at the top." When I was in college, I was extremely active in student government. By the end of my junior year, I was elected as the first woman student-body president our university had ever had. The four years I spent organizing, planning, and leading were exciting, but they were also often lonely. One particular night I wrote in my journal, "Everyone turns out for the concerts, parties, and banquets we plan. And everyone has a great time. But there sure is a difference between planning the activity and being part of it. I feel as though I'm merely standing on the outside looking in."

This type of loneliness often attacks those in positions of spiritual leadership. Take the Old Testament prophet Elijah. God did incredible things through this man. He defeated the army of Baal (and the odds were 450 to one!), he stood up against King Ahab, and he led thousands to believe in and worship the Lord.

Yet after the big Baal bash, he withdrew into the mountains and asked God to let him die. He complained that he was the only godly man left. Loneliness always seems to intensify when we can't find others who share our beliefs. The Lord opened Elijah's spiritual eyes a little wider and revealed to him that there were actually *seven thousand* godly people around him. When you're experiencing this kind of loneliness, ask God to reveal those around you who share your standards and values.

4. *Loneliness caused by society.* We live in such a fast-paced, technological world that everyone has been reduced to a number. Even though we carry a collection of cards with our

names on them, it's really our number that's important. When you're pulled over by a police officer, he calls in your number. When you charge a new pair of shoes at the mall, it's the number off your credit card the store wants. These kinds of incidents tend to make us feel as though we're living in a very impersonal world, with no one really caring who we are.

5. *Loneliness caused by a particular path we've chosen or a specific decision we've made.* This isn't saying we've chosen to be alone or sad, but because we've chosen to go against the flow, we feel isolated.

For instance, maybe you've become a Christian against your family's wishes. It's understandable why you'd feel alone; you're receiving no emotional support from those closest to you.

Likewise, when we take a stand for purity or morality, we often feel lonely because we've decided to go against what the majority believe. We expect to get a negative reaction from the world. After all, they don't share our conscience. They're not striving to live a holy life. But what really hurts is when we're ridiculed by one another. Oftentimes people in the church will criticize each other for taking a stand. Instead of causing dissension, we need to be holding each other up, supporting one another, and affirming those around us.

This happened to me when I went to college. I was brought up in a conservative family who did not attend movies. During my growing-up years, my non-Christian friends never gave me a hard time about that. They simply accepted it. It was when I enrolled in a Christian college that my Christian friends questioned and berated my decision. "You don't go to movies? You've got to be kidding. That's ridiculous!" Again, as believers, we need to encourage each other.

Our Lord felt this kind of loneliness in the Garden of Gethsemane. Though he brought three disciples with him, he went farther than they did. While they stayed behind, Jesus went farther physically, emotionally, and spiritually. Only he could communicate with God at this particular point in his life.

There comes a time in all of our lives when we too must choose to go farther spiritually than those around us. After all, you alone will answer to God about your spiritual depth. This type of loneliness is essential in a growing Christian's life.

———— ·◇· ————

Everyone experiences loneliness. Some loneliness actually strengthens our character while other types of loneliness accentuate our aloneness. During the "alone" times—when you're craving the company of others—concentrate on specific things you can do to significantly curb these solo feelings.

PICK A PET

There's a reason psychiatrists and doctors encourage singles, elderly people, and those who are ill to buy a pet. It's simply because everyone needs to love and to be loved. I cherish the thought of knowing my golden retriever, Jamaica, is waiting for me when I come through the door each evening.

I need her. She's the only one giving me a generous supply of "hugs" and kisses each day. We all need hugs. But we can't tell people that—they'll think we're starved for attention. (Though I do have a couple of close friends I often confide in, saying, "I need a hug.") A pet can certainly help alleviate the loneliness.

FIND A FAMILY

Singles are usually segregated in churches and social functions. If you're visiting a church and are greeted by someone at the door, as soon as they find out you're single, they direct you to the singles' class. And that's sometimes good, but sometimes bad. What if you want to interact with couples or families?

Though I definitely need friendships with other singles, I have come to realize that I also need to be plugged into a few families. Living away from my own family leaves me yearning for another unit.

I've moved a few times during the past ten years, and every time I do, I begin praying early for a family in my new city—people who will love and accept me and allow me to be a part of their lives.

Where can you find a family? Although there are possibilities at work, I've found the closest relationships I establish are always from church. So whenever I move, my first goal is to find a church I can plug into.

My first full-time position after college was as a youth minister six hours away from my hometown. I moved to Conway, Arkansas, alone. I traded in a large group of college friends for a handful of junior high and high school kids: from the electric buzz of dorm life to the emptiness of a three-bedroom house. It was an adjustment.

A couple of months passed and I became friends with a woman in the church who was ten years older than I. She was married and had four kids. One evening she invited me over for dinner. When I arrived, the kids were setting the table and she was putting the finishing touches on our food. She then walked me into the dining room and showed me where I would sit.

"This is your place," she said. "It will always be your place. We want you to be a part of our family. So every evening there will always be a place set for you right here. Understand what I'm saying, Susie. *This place will always be set for you.* You're not going to come over and watch us scramble to set an extra place. We will always set this place for you. If you get a better offer, fine; you're not obligated to come over every night. But we want you. So anytime you walk through the door, feel comfortable knowing your place is always set; there will always be an extra helping."

Do you know what that did for me? For a green twenty-one-year-old fresh out of college and away from home for the first time, it gave me a deep sense of belonging. They took time to make my birthdays special and even hung up a stocking with my name on it at Christmastime. Their love and involvement in my life affected me in an indescribable way!

And, yes, today, seventeen years later, we're still as close as we've ever been. I gained a family for life.

About six months after coming to Colorado Springs, I became friends with my pastor's family. And about four months later, our pastor's wife gave me a key to their house. Cheryl explained, "You're a part of our family, Susie. Come over when you want. It's okay if we're not here. Use our house to make yourself at home."

Again, it gave me a sense of belonging. We need that. Everyone needs to feel included, a part of something. I know I have somewhere to go for dinner when my fridge is empty, people to talk things over with when life gets too hectic, and a place to go when I just don't want to be alone for the evening.

Many times on a Friday evening, Cheryl will call and say, "Bring your dog over and spend the night." Jamaica and I will take over the entire basement—but only after playing several games of UNO with their kids and watching a video or two.

And when the church has those all-family potluck dinners, Cheryl knows how uncomfortable I feel about walking in alone. Without fail, she pulls me aside and says, "Remember, you're part of our family. We want you to go with us, help us carry our food in, and sit with us. No need to bring anything. I've got you covered."

The apprehension I feel about having to cook something or walking in alone and trying to find a table with a few empty chairs left is immediately taken care of ... because now *I belong to a family!*

Let me encourage you to spend some time praying for a family to love. Our creative God has such a variety of ways to fill the void in our lives when we seek his help.

Start praying now for God to begin preparing the hearts of some special people for you. You may or may not have any idea who they'll be. As you continue to make this an important priority in your prayer life, God will either begin bringing people into your life who are approachable, warm, and accepting, or begin opening your eyes to some people you may already know but haven't thought of in this way. As you observe them more closely, you'll feel more and more comfortable about approaching them.

GIVE AWAY TO GET

I've found that as I concentrate on giving to others, it helps me forget about the emptiness in my own life. I look for opportunities to do something for couples or families at church. A few weeks ago I called a young married couple from my Sunday school class and asked if I could bring supper over on Saturday evening.

My friend Shirley was delighted. "Bring Jamaica, too!" she said. I gathered my casserole, salad, cake, and golden retriever and headed downtown. After dinner and TV, they begged me to bunk on the couch and spend the night. I didn't, but it proves couples want to be friends with singles—they enjoy our company. Most of them just don't know how to initiate a friendship with one when they're used to socializing with two.

I recently invited three couples over for an evening of dinner and games. I was the only single. After lasagne, I announced that I had created a game similar to "The Newlywed Game" and each couple would be competing against the other two.

To make things even more fun, I had baked homemade bread for each couple as a prize for being in the game, and had a grand prize for the winners. I sent the guys downstairs until I had asked the three wives the first round of questions. The husbands came upstairs and tried to match answers. Afterward, we switched, and I sent the women downstairs and asked the men a round of questions.

It was hilarious getting to learn some inside fun facts about each couple, and each couple had fun getting to know the others better. Everyone had a great time, and I felt good that I had not resorted to simply having people over who were single and people I was used to hanging out with.

TREAT YOURSELF TO TRADITION

Why not create a few traditions for yourself? We tend to think traditions are only for families, but we can establish traditions as individuals, and can also create traditions for other families.

Every Christmas I buy myself a new ornament for the tree. I've never purchased a tree, but, boy, do I have the ornaments! Since I fly home every Christmas, I've never bothered to decorate my house, but I know someday I will, and when I do—I'm ready!

Buying an ornament has become a fun tradition for me that I enjoy. It's exciting to seek out just the right decoration each year—one that I'll associate with specific memories during the past few months and treasure for years to come.

I've also started a few traditions with others. For instance, with my pastor's family, I suggested we have a "Triple F Night" once a month. It stands for "Friday Family Fun Night." We plan to do something special—sometimes it costs money; other times it doesn't.

We might go out to dinner, then back to the house for a video. Or we might just make a fire and roast marshmallows and play games. What we do isn't as important as doing it together and having a specific time to have fun.

Are there some traditions you can create for yourself? What about for others? It helps fill the void when you're busying yourself in the fulfillment of other people's lives.

GET INVOLVED

There are several other ways and places to get involved, but I've found my interaction in the lives of people in my church fills a social need and helps keep me spiritually accountable. Plus, the church has so many areas of need.

Think about it. You can help with the youth group, senior citizens, or nursery, sing in the choir, start a drama team, join the visitation crew, or participate in many other areas of service.

Mike and I have chosen to get involved with a family in our church who has three boys. Mike has almost adopted the teen boy as his "little bro," and I've recruited the mom to help me with skits in our church services. Her husband recently lost his job. The family was devastated. Since Dodie is a stay-at-home mom, financial tension quickly surfaced.

Mike and I wanted to do something to show that we cared. We knew they probably wouldn't want to go anywhere since during times of stress most people want to hang close to home—a security and financial issue. So we brought dinner to them. We pooled our money and picked up large buckets of chicken, corn on the cob, potatoes and gravy, biscuits, baked beans, and dessert (three growing boys eat a lot!) and spent the evening just loving this special family.

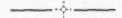

Loneliness is no respecter of persons. Everyone experiences it. You might try all the above suggestions and still feel completely alone. Or you may be surrounded by friends, family, and collegues and still feel lonely.

An eleven-year-old boy left for camp. This was his first camping experience and he was uneasy about leaving home. At the end of his first day, he sent a letter home to his parents that read:

> Dear Mom and Dad,
>
> There are fifty boys here at camp. I *wish* there were only forty-nine.

Do you feel that way? Take comfort in knowing that the greatest men of all time—and the spiritual heroes of the Old and New Testaments—felt that way too. Take a fresh peek at the Psalms. More than once, David cries out in despair and loneliness to his Father. At one point he screams that no one is around. This is David talking! The anointed one. The king. He was constantly surrounded by servants attending to his needs and friends supporting his decisions, yet he felt alone. The apostle Paul in the last chapter of his final letter to Timothy laments that everyone has forsaken him.

Some of the greatest contributions to the kingdom of God have been made by people who experienced deep loneliness.

Let me propose a new twist. Instead of being lost in despair, think of loneliness as a gift to God. In doing so, we automatically remove the negative connotations associated with loneliness and turn it into something positive.

I'm striving to present my loneliness as a gift to my heavenly Father. It's during these times that we can deepen our relationship with him. Sometimes it takes being alone to really solidify our theology and strengthen our spiritual muscles. He loves us so much that he uses our loneliness to draw us closer to him. What a gift!

CHAPTER 3

What Churches Can Do to Include Singles

My home church has an annual "Singles Appreciation Week." The 2,500-member congregation is encouraged to treat singles in the church to lunch, write them encouraging notes, and make a special effort to let them know how much they are loved.

Even though I live thirteen hours away from home, I've heard from some of my single friends how terrific it makes them feel. "For an entire week," Brenda said, "we're the focus of everyone's attention. It's terrific!"

My parents treated Andrea and Karen to Sunday lunch after church and called them during the week. Other families included singles in regular outings and activities.

BECOMING AWARE

If it feels as though you're on the outside looking in at your church, perhaps you simply need to help your congregation become aware of singles' needs. I've come to realize that most churches don't purposely exclude singles—they just don't think about specific ways of making the solo crowd feel more at home with the church family.

Many churches often have potluck dinners in which everyone is alphabetically assigned to bring something. This often gags a single. When realizing they're expected to bring, say, a meat dish, they'll opt not to attend.

My church always adds a clause at the end of the list: "Singles bring a dozen rolls." Whew! That's pretty easy. I can quickly run to the grocery store and grab a bag of rolls, I think.

And what about those tables? Ever notice how every table has an even number of chairs? Suggest placing an odd number of seats at each table. This way a single person won't feel as though he or she is taking up a married couple's spot, and it will force everyone to include an uneven number of people at each table.

SINGLES SENSATION

If your church doesn't have an active singles group, perhaps you can be instrumental in starting one. Enola, a young single woman in the church Mike and I attend, works hard to create several options for our singles. And what's most exciting about her efforts is that she helps focus the attention of singles toward others.

A few years back, she started an annual tradition called "The Senior Prom." Every spring, the singles throw a first-class banquet for the senior citizens in the congregation. They provide the entertainment, food, and chauffeur service. It's little wonder that the over-sixty-five crowd loves this group of singles! They're treated like gold and are extremely appreciative. Besides helping singles focus on the needs of others, this also works to create a warm bond between the two age groups. Once the older adults get to know the single crowd, they return the favors with countless dinner invitations and consistent prayer.

Enola and her singles' council also instigated a church staff appreciation dinner this year. They sent formal invitations to each staff person and spouse and told them to dress in their Sunday clothes. Child care, would be provided.

Enola and the singles group rented three limos ($40 an hour per limo) and had a single ride in each limo. On the big day, staff members were picked up between 5:30 and 6:00 P.M.

A single met the staff couple at their door, presented the wife with a half dozen roses, and escorted them to the limo. They were then chauffeured to a beautiful home owned by a family in the church, where they were greeted with sparkling cider and hors d'oeuvres.

A musician played soft dinner music on a grand piano in an adjoining room, and a chef was hired ($50) to prepare a five-course dinner. Singles waited on the tables, poured beverages, and provided light entertainment.

After dessert, singles gathered around each couple and shared specific reasons why they appreciated them. As the staff exited, each was given a goodie basket filled with home-made bread, candy, jellies, and tea. People in the church arrived at 8:45 to shuttle them home.

You can guess that our church staff talked about this event for months! But they weren't the only ones. The singles still reflect on that special evening when they gave so completely of themselves to make others feel important.

BASHING THE HOLIDAY BLUES

The holidays are often a tough time for singles because our singleness is enhanced. Bethany First Nazarene Church, near Oklahoma City, has an annual activity called "Home for the Holidays." The church has sponsored this event for years, and singles everywhere turn out for this classy evening.

It's a semi-formal occasion with first-class entertainment. A full-course holiday meal of ham and turkey is always served. Singles from that area have learned to expect a time of fun, fellowship, and "class" during this special evening.

INVOLVE US WITH FAMILIES!

We've said this before, and we can't say it enough: As singles, we want to be included in a family! We can help churches learn to integrate us with families. But we must not forget that we can also take responsibility to feel part of the church. We can't just sit around thinking, *How come the Smiths never have me over for dinner?*

For about eight months I had been wanting to get to know Brian and Diane, a couple close to my age in my church. One Sunday, I simply approached them and said, "Can I bring a bucket of Kentucky Fried Chicken for dinner sometime this week?" They loved the idea! I was immediately invited over for an opportunity to get to know them better.

That was about a year ago. After a few fun dinners, we quickly became friends and now do several things together.

Many times, though, activities planned for singles will be organized in a single's home or apartment. Churches can help singles feel more included by encouraging married couples or families to open their homes for singles' activities such as a potato bar after church, mini-pizzas on English muffins, burger grills, etc. The more we get inside homes of married people and families, the more we feel connected.

THEY'RE TRYING

Even though many churches are trying to reach out to singles, and granted, some are determined to make us feel welcome, still there are a few well-meaning adults who always say the wrong things.

Again, it's a matter of helping to educate the married crowd about the needs and unique feelings we singles have. In order to help your married friends understand your singleness better, pass along the following suggestions excerpted from an article by Susan Maycinik which first appeared in the 1994 May/June issue of *Discipleship Journal.* Though it's geared to women, men will enjoy it as well.

Top 10 Things *Not* to Say to a Single

"You never married, did you?" I was mingling at a gathering of my relatives when my mother's cousin's second wife startled me with this inquiry. It was more a statement than a question. *Never married, past tense?* I thought. *I guess she thinks there's no hope for me!* Yet I was only 32 at the time!

I gathered my composure, smiled sweetly and told her about the Air Force officer I was dating. Just minutes later, in a different conversation, a distant cousin (who'd married her high school sweetheart) commented, "You never married, did you?"

By then, the absurdity struck me, and I had to chuckle inwardly. Most of my high school girlfriends had married before they hit 20. At 30-plus, I *must* have seemed, to my relatives, like a confirmed "spinster"!

No harm was done that day. But I remember other instances when innocent comments by married women *did* hurt. In many cases, they were trying to be encouraging. But because they had forgotten (or had never known) what it was like to wait for a husband year after year, their comments felt like stabs in an already-aching heart.

I'm not alone. As I've talked with dozens of still-single women, I've discovered we've heard many of the same lines from our married acquaintances and friends. Most of them are well-intentioned, but they have an underlying message that makes us cringe.

1. *"As soon as you're content, God will bring a man into your life."*

Granted, there's a hint of truth in this one. Some women *do* scare men off because they're so desperate to get married. But slapping this saying on every single woman is insensitive.

The "just be content" line and its close relative, "just have faith"—trivialize the struggle many of us have to accept singleness. God has built into nearly every woman I've met a deep longing to have someone to share her life with. When that desire goes unfulfilled for five, 10, 15 years or more—when it begins to look like it will *never* be fulfilled—the pain can be intense. Telling a single woman to "just be content" shows her you know little of her struggle.

What's more, this statement implies there's a formula to follow that will guarantee you'll soon be walking down the aisle. Conversely, if you're not married, you must be doing something wrong. Not true.

God's plan for each woman—including if and when she marries—is unique. God's not a vending machine, dispensing a husband when enough contentment coins are inserted. He doesn't withhold His blessings until we deserve them.

I loved it when Sarah, who married for the first time at 34, told the truth about this myth. "Did you have to learn how to be content before you met Michael?" a single woman asked her. She laughed. "I tried that," she said, "and it didn't work! I was still really struggling with singleness when we began dating."

2. "Before you find someone wonderful, you've got to be someone wonderful."

We've all heard this platitude from well-meaning speakers at singles' functions. A woman who was discipling my friend Deena had another version: "Before you find your prince, you've got to be a princess."

Deena's mentor thought she was encouraging her to grow spiritually. Instead, her comment led to despair.

"It seemed like something I could never attain," Deena said. "Plus, it communicated that whether or not I got married rested on me. What if I couldn't be good enough?"

Like the admonition to be content, this statement communicates, "You're not married because there's something wrong with you," or, "You don't deserve anyone yet." So does speculating aloud that your friend must be single because God still has work to do in her life. God doesn't reward us with a husband for spiritual maturity!

Obviously, some very godly women never marry. And many women who have quite a lot of growing to do find partners at an early age. Help your friend grow when you see areas of weakness. But don't give her the message that her chance for matrimony depends on her progress!

3. "You're too picky."

Home for the holidays, my childhood friend and I were sitting in her parents' kitchen discussing life. She had married at 18. When her mother overheard me explaining how hard it was to meet desirable men, she tossed off this concise assessment of my problem. *How would you know?* I thought. *You have no idea what the men I know are like. And besides, you haven't dated for more than 40 years!*

Many married women think singles must be too picky because they imagine the dating scene to be like it was for them in high school or college. They assume there's an unlimited supply of available men, and a woman who can't find someone must be too selective.

But as a woman leaves her mid–20s, the situation changes drastically. She may not meet Christian men in her office or at the health club. Some churches do have singles groups, but often these groups attract emotionally unhealthy men—or those who have no interest in following Jesus. I know many attractive, outgoing, godly women who have gone for years at a time without being asked for a date.

There may be a few women out there who are still looking for a handsome, witty, athletic, romantic, dynamic spiritual leader who could support a family on one income and talk easily about his feelings. But most of us just want to meet a man who loves God, whom we enjoy being around and who is at least taking a stab at a career. Is that too much to ask?

4. *"Are you seeing anyone special?"*

If your friend is dating someone, you'll hear about him! If she isn't, you've just brought up a sore subject. It may make her feel stupid to have to answer no to that question for what seems like the hundredth time. She senses that you want her to say yes, and that she's failed somehow. It's like asking a woman who's been struggling with infertility for years, "Are you pregnant yet?" Why not simply ask your single friend what she's been doing lately? That gives her a chance to focus on what's positive in her life, not what's missing.

5. *"If you'd just lose weight ..."*

Jeane commented at her friend's bridal shower that she wished she could date more. The tall, willowy bride-to-be responded, "Well, if you'd lose 25 pounds, more men would ask you out."

Injured, Jeane asked, "You mean to tell me that if God brought a man into my life, he wouldn't want me now?"

"No, he wouldn't," her friend said. "I'm just being honest because I care about you."

Jeane told me later, "I felt as though she were saying God would only bless thin women—that I was so flawed, no man would *ever* want me."

Another friend echoed her comments. "All my life people have been telling me, 'You have such a pretty face. If only you'd lose weight. . . .' That's supposed to be a compliment?"

The women who suggested weight loss *were* trying to help. They'd observed that a lot of men—including Christian men—*do* judge a book by its cover. But it's harmful to suggest to a single friend that no man could accept her as she is.

6. *"Getting married doesn't solve all your problems."*

Around the time I turned 30, I went through a grieving process over my dream of having a husband and family. Sometimes I would try to tell other women about my loneliness and disappointment. More than once, a married woman responded somewhat impatiently, "Well, getting married doesn't solve all your problems!" Some added the tired corollary, "It just gives you new ones!"

That condescending response communicates two things: (1) "I don't care how you're feeling," and (2), "You don't have a clue what marriage involves."

I don't think any woman really thinks that when she finds a husband, her problems disappear. If she has married friends, she's well aware of the struggles and frustrations on the other side of the altar. Most of us don't dismiss lightly what we'd be giving up to become a wife and mother. Yet many of us would gladly choose a more difficult life and someone to share it with over a simpler life alone.

7. *"You're such a wonderful person. I can't believe you're not married."*

What's wrong with this statement? It's a subtle put-down of a woman's marital status. Imagine how you'd feel if a single woman said to you, "You're such a wonderful person. I can't believe you got married!"

If you want to affirm a single woman, why not leave it at, "You're such a wonderful person!"

8. *"Why haven't you ever married?"*

Well, that's what many of us would like to know! Why hasn't God given us husbands when so many other women have one?

We may come up with an answer if we look at things from a human perspective: "I'm shy and men don't notice me." "My advanced degree intimidates guys." "I always seem to be attracted to the wrong men." Even, "I'm too tall."

But only God knows the real reason for our singleness. He may have someone for us a few (or more than a few) years down the road. He may want us to minister to the growing population of singles. He may want to keep us free from the distractions of marriage

(1 Corinthians 7:32–35). Or, He may want to build something into our character that only singleness can accomplish.

Please don't ask us why we're not married. In many cases, singleness isn't our choice.

9. *"You need to let Jesus meet your needs."*

Certainly Jesus is the true Lover of our soul. If we think a husband will satisfy our deepest longings, we're sadly mistaken. We *all* need to grow in turning to the Lord first to meet our needs.

But before you quote Isaiah 54:5 to your friend ("Your Maker is your husband"), consider this: As the late psychologist Bill Crabb pointed out, in the Garden of Eden, Adam had perfect, unbroken fellowship with God. Yet God said, "It is not good for the man to be alone" (Genesis 2:18). God never intended for His fellowship to be enough! He created human relationships, including marriage, to meet some of our relational needs.

Don't imply to your friend that if she were just spiritual enough, being single wouldn't bother her. Encourage her to grow closer to Jesus, to let Him be her Best Friend—and to reach out to other Christian friends for companionship. But accept the fact that as long as she's single, some healthy, important longings will go unmet, and that will be hard.

10. *"God has someone picked out especially for you. You just need to wait."*

Most women wouldn't dream of telling a friend, "God is going to cure your cancer," or "Don't worry—you *will* be able to conceive." Yet some are certain they can predict the future in this area.

An elderly couple I spoke with at a missions conference assured me that God had a partner for everyone. "Why," one of them gushed, "we have a friend who married for the first time when she was 63!" (The thought of waiting 30 more years didn't exactly fill me with joy!)

Though it would be nice to believe that everyone will marry eventually, it just isn't true. People I've met from all over the country—married and single—have observed that there are simply more women who are emotionally healthy, committed to Christ, and who want to get married than there are men.

Telling a woman that God has someone for her may be building a false hope. It may also influence her to focus on the wrong goals. When a young woman sees herself only as a future wife and mother, she may never develop her gifts in other areas. She may also face bitter disappointment when she discovers the role she's been preparing for all her life just isn't available.

THE GIFT OF HOPE

Singles go through many stages in their feelings about singleness. Some hardly ever think about it. But for others, singleness can be excruciating. Women may feel as if men have rejected them, God has betrayed them, and the most important dream of their life will never come true.

At thirty-six, I've come to the point where I'm usually at peace with being single. I'm overwhelmed by how God is using and blessing me, and I'm excited about my life! But about a month ago, those painful feelings of anger and hopelessness came rushing back after a serious dating relationship ended suddenly.

My married friend Lorraine caught me on a particularly bad day. She sat and listened as I vented my pain and confusion. She admitted she didn't know the answers either. She reminded me that Jesus knew how I felt and wanted to comfort me.

Then, after I'd gone through a pile of tissues and poured out everything that was in my heart, she said just the right thing. "What else are you passionate about?" she asked, leaning forward in her chair. "What other dreams do you have—besides marriage and a family—that make your heart beat faster?"

Drying my eyes, I began to think. "I want to work on sharing Christ with my neighbors. And I'm really excited about training Christian writers and editors in other countries. Oh, and there are some articles that I've been wanting to write . . ."

"What can you do right now about those dreams?" she prodded. We began to brainstorm. Lorraine gave me two gifts that day. She accepted me as I was. And she helped me see that while one of my dreams is on hold, there are other important, fulfilling dreams that I can pursue. Lorraine gave me hope.

Our married friends' words can hurt us. But, guided by the Holy Spirit, they can also be God's instruments of healing.

WORDS WE LOVE TO HEAR

What are some things you should say to encourage your single friend?

1. *"Tell me about your job."* In too many women's gatherings, conversation centers around husbands and children. Single women feel left out. We love to get the chance to talk about the important things in our lives. Ask us not only what we do but what we like most about our job and what our dreams are for our careers. Ask us about our hobbies, too!

2. *"Sometimes I envy you."* It's easy to fall into the trap of focusing on what we *don't* have. You can help us see—and celebrate—the good things we'd have to give up if we married.

3. "Do you want to go shopping with me on Saturday?" Singles appreciate anything that lets us into others' lives, whether that be an invitation to come for dinner or a request to pray with you. Ask us to be a friend—we'd love it!

4. "God is big enough." Many times, when we look around us, it seems certain that we'll always be alone. Remind us that our powerful and loving God is much bigger than our circumstances. Tell us about the miracles in your life, the "impossible" situations in which God has intervened. Help us focus on God.

5. "You're really special. Your friendship means a lot to me." It's a rare person who doesn't, at some time, experience perpetual singleness as rejection. Tell us what you like about us, how you've seen us grow, and why you're proud of us. Let us know you want to be around us.

Recent statistics have shown that almost one-half of the population of the United States is single. Single Christians can indeed make significant contributions in their churches and in their neighborhoods, spreading the Gospel and volunteering in their communities in organizations such as Big Brothers/Sisters, Right-to-Life, and others. They can also serve on church boards and committees, teach, and mentor new Christians.

Churches need to address the needs of singles by incorporating them into the family of God, welcoming them as whole persons, complete as they are.

CHAPTER 4

Sparking Friendships
With the Opposite Sex

Everyone needs friends! When you're not involved in a dating relationship, consider using this special time to focus on strengthening your friendships with the opposite sex.

Girls need guys they can count on for friendship—someone who can fix clogged drains, help test-drive new cars, and simply care for them.

Guys need female friends who can go shopping with them, tell them what looks great, and when to keep looking, and who'll occasionally have them over for a bowl of homemade stew. Most important, they need someone they can share their heart with—especially when their dating life goes awry.

Without trying to turn your friends of the opposite sex into dates, learn to value and treasure their suggestions concerning your life. You'll be much richer because of it.

———————— N W–◇–E S ————————

Greg fixed my broken cabinet door. Woodie went with me to purchase my new car. Stanley followed me home and walked me through the house when I was getting obscene phone calls. Brian fixed my front bumper for me. And I called

Mike at 4 A.M. once when I saw the neighbor's porch light go on and knew they were living in Phoenix for six months.

I can't help but laugh when I think of the fun, silly things Mike and I have done together. When we lived in southern California, we went to a taping of TV's "Designing Women." It started at 6 P.M., but because each scene was done about three times, we were still in the studio audience at 8:30.

A comedian had been hired to entertain us between takes and was trying to fill time by enlisting audience volunteers to tell jokes. He promised the best joke would receive a "Designing Women" T-shirt.

For more than an hour I had frantically waved my hand in the air, but I seemed to be invisible to this guy. Neither Mike nor I had had supper, and he was getting fidgety. "Let's get out of here and hit that Chinese place we both like," he kept saying. Though that *did* sound good, I wasn't about to leave until I'd had my chance at temporary "stand-up" comedy.

"Mike, help me get this guy's attention! As soon as I tell my joke and win the T-shirt, we can leave."

So Mike began enlisting the help of strangers seated around us, and after the next take, the comedian once again called for volunteers. This time when I raised my hand, our entire section yelled, "Hey! She's got a joke!" Obviously, I was chosen, but by the time I reached the front of the stands, another scene was in progress. We had to wait another fifteen minutes. Two scenes later, I saw my opportunity and grabbed the microphone. With the lights in my face and a captive studio audience, I suddenly came to life!

I told my joke; Mike forced everyone in our section to vote *me* best joke teller; I was awarded the coveted pink T-shirt; we grabbed it and literally ran out of the building while the comedian angrily screamed after us, "Oh, sure! As soon as you get something free, you take off!"

Mike, gasping for breath and salivating for wontons, screamed back, "You got *that* right, buddy!"

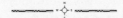

In addition to the fun times I share with Susie, I enjoy getting together with my pal Jan. (Who says members of the opposite sex can't just be friends?) In fact, Jan and I have designated each other as "shoulder pals."

Whenever she's having a tough time in a relationship and needs a male perspective—and a shoulder to cry on—Jan rings my number or knocks on my door. Likewise, she's there for me.

I'll never forget when she and I shed a few tears together at the movie "Sleepless in Seattle." (Yes, guys do cry at theaters . . . we just don't admit it.)

"Why can't we find that kind of love in real life?" I asked Jan afterward, as we sat in a restaurant. "For the past few weeks, I've been going out with a woman my friends introduced me to, but I feel like Meg Ryan's character. I'm unsure if I even want to pursue this relationship. She has a lot of qualities a guy could want. Yet something doesn't feel right. I'm very unsure about the whole thing."

Jan nodded and took a sip of her soft drink. "Andrew and I haven't been getting along lately, either. I just don't understand him . . . or what's on his mind. Come to think of it, I don't understand men, period."

"Hey, I don't understand women."

"Is dating supposed to be this hard?"

"Beats me."

"Think we'll ever find the right person?"

"I don't know. Hey, do you want the rest of that pie?"

Jan flashed a smile, then shoved her plate across the table. We spent the rest of the evening moaning a bit but laughing a lot. Our time together took our minds off our pain and gave us fresh perspectives for tackling our troubles.

MAKING MAGICAL MEMORIES

But more than calling on a friend of the opposite sex when you need him/her, strive to cultivate fun, social moments together. You know what that does? It provides wonderful memories to fall back on when life gets tough.

Another memory with Mike that always makes me smile is the time we were invited to visit Steven Spielberg's studios, Amblin Entertainment. Before you start thinking, *Wow! They know Spielberg!* let me fill you in.

We probably wouldn't know the movie mogul if we passed him in the hall, but his assistant is a personal friend of our friend Greg. She invited Greg to stop by the studio after hours to see the place, and Mike and I begged Greg to let us come too. (Okay, we bribed him.) Anyway, we piled into Greg's car and headed for Hollywood after work.

It was incredible! We walked right into Spielberg's office, saw the original mechanical E.T., oohed over the original Roger Rabbit, were treated to snacks in his private screening room, played all kinds of video games in the lounge, and, of course, hung around in his office taking pictures of ourselves sitting behind his desk.

That's when Mike got the bright idea of going into Spielberg's private bathroom. Now, I'll sit at someone's desk or look to see if I know the people in the photos there. Maybe I'll even scribble on someone else's personalized memo pad—but snoop in someone's *bathroom?* That's going too far.

Not for Mike. Greg and Jamie had left the office and were headed toward the opposite end of the building. Mike saw his opportunity and grabbed my camera.

"Susie, quick! Let's take a shot of his bathroom."

"No way, Mike! That's weird. Give me back my camera."

"No! I want a picture of the bathroom."

"Well, you're not getting it. Come on! They're going to wonder where we are."

"I'm not leaving till you take a shot of me standing by the sink."

"No! It's *my* camera. Give it back!"

"I'm serious, Susie. You'll never see this camera again if you don't take my picture."

Little beads of sweat were standing out on his brow. I knew he was serious. I had to consent. He then grabbed Spielberg's bottle of mouthwash and coerced me into shooting him spitting it down the sink.

Is it any wonder during deadline crunch, when the pressure starts to build, that I often think back on that special memory and laugh out loud.

FRIENDSHIP TREASURES

The sign of true friendship is when the other person can let his or her hair down and not worry about what you think. And you know your friendship is especially solid when you can do dumb things and not be laughed at. Regardless of what you do, the other person still accepts you and introduces you to others as "my good friend" (and vice versa).

All of us need special fun times with friends of the opposite sex that we can reflect on and laugh about during stressful days. So before you flip on to the next adventure, let us remind you of three things we're trying to incorporate.

1. If you want to be rich . . .

Friends of the opposite sex make our lives richer, more fulfilling, and much more well-rounded. They also help us continue our social development. But most important of all, opposite gender pals are valuable keys to understanding the opposite sex. They can help you figure out what your dating partner may be thinking and how you can be more effective in meeting his or her needs.

2. If you want to break some myths . . .

Don't believe the myth that single men and women can't be friends without involving their hormones. It's not only possible, but we encourage you to establish some good, old-fashioned, fun, platonic friendships with singles of the opposite sex.

3. If you want a different perspective . . .

Women, there are times when you need a male's perspective. Perhaps your boyfriend just broke off your six-month dating relationship. Chances are, after you've cried with seven of your best girlfriends, you'll want to hear a guy's perspective.

Have a Coke with a guy friend and share your dilemma: "I don't know what happened! I was perfect for him. I baked him enough bread to last a whole month. I took him just-out-of-the-oven dinners at work. I got a key from his landlord and cleaned his entire apartment when he was gone . . . and even bought him a new suit! So, what did I do wrong?!"

A trustworthy male friend can offer insight and a fresh, objective perspective that you might be missing.

And guys, once in a while, you need to be reminded of a woman's viewpoint. It's okay to sit down with a female friend and unload what's inside: "I just don't understand what went wrong! Our dates were a blast. We went hiking, bowling, rappelling, four-wheeling, and I even took her to the batting cages. Go figure!"

Sparking up friendships with the opposite sex can be beneficial and rewarding. Friends of the opposite sex can offer insight into relationships with dating partners. They can also come in handy when we need chaperones or helpers around the house. If we want companionship or someone on which to unload life's stressors, who better to call than a trusted friend who accepts us as we are.

PART TWO:

Dating, Waiting and Finding a Mate

CHAPTER 5

Attracting a Mate Without Being Obvious

I'd finally landed a date with Eilene—a woman I really wanted to impress. To me, she seemed like the ideal person . . . she liked my kind of music, she was zany and fun, and, most importantly, she loved the outdoors.

"Yes, yes, yes . . . ooohhh, YES!" I screamed as I slammed the receiver and broke into a "victory" dance. We had decided to go horseback riding at her uncle's ranch. "She likes me! Next Saturday, it's off to the mountains with Eilene!"

I didn't think anything could possibly go wrong. I imagined both of us riding side-by-side through a peaceful valley filled with little creatures like Bambi and Thumper.

It'll be the ultimate in romance, I thought. *I'll gently take her hand and we'll both ride into the sunset together.*

But there was one tiny little detail I overlooked: I had never been on a horse in my life. I had ridden a donkey at an amusement park once when I was ten—but never a horse on steep mountain trails.

No problem, I thought. *I've seen lots of John Wayne movies. I'll just imitate the Duke. She'll think I was born on a stallion!*

That Saturday, after being chased by a pack of scrubby-looking dogs and nearly thrown off Chester, my spooked horse, I suddenly realized I had a serious problem. Here I was, screaming at the top of my lungs, bouncing like a yo-yo on a string as I clung to the back of this frightened beast. And it seemed like old Chester—who was prime glue-factory material—reached unheard of speeds as he galloped down hills, through dry riverbeds, and under low-hanging branches.

"Michael! Are you okay? You could have been killed!" Eilene yelled when she caught up to us. She began to calm Chester. I slithered off the horse and hugged the ground for awhile.

"Huh? Yeah, I'm fine. How about if we just walk the horses through that safe meadow, then head back to your uncle's place," I suggested.

Big mistake!

By this time, I was an emotional mess. I couldn't talk or walk—at least like a human. I resembled a bowlegged chimp and I sounded like one, too. Sadly enough, my dating nightmare didn't end here.

As we made our way through a field, a long, green grasshopper decided to wander across my sneakers, up one of my legs and into my pants. I didn't detect the little guy until he reached my back pocket. Then I let out a bloodcurdling yell and began to swat wildly at my jeans.

Eilene looked on in horror. She never went out with me again.

———— ✦ ————

Dating blunders. Trying too hard to live up to an expectation that no human can attain. Crashing conversations. First impressions that seem to bomb. Sound familiar?

It all spells the same thing: I-N-S-E-C-U-R-I-T-Y.

But whether we like it or not, ours is a society of packaging. Sadly, first impressions count. Even if you're the hippest single on the face of this earth—and really deserve a chance with your date—you won't get past first base if insecurity gets in the way.

Let's focus our attention on a tip some people already know: You have to "package" yourself if you're even going to have a chance.

Now, I know what you're thinking: *Hold up. Why should Christians have to do that? Shouldn't people just accept us the way we are? "Packaging" sounds like deception.*

Actually, it's not. What I'm talking about is putting your best foot forward—and that's just plain smart, not to mention practical. The first impression you make comes from your appearance.

A single friend once told me: "It's not merely the way you comb your hair. Your appearance also involves body language: facial expressions (smiles or frowns), the position of your body, how you walk . . . and confidence that comes from the inside. It's a self-transformation strategy."

So how can you blast through the dating jitters, put your best foot forward, and achieve a happy end to your adventure in singlehood? Try this four-point plan. It isn't necessarily a ticket to matrimony, but it's a practical way to polish your package. And that will boost your self-esteem.

STEP #1: ATTITUDE IS EVERYTHING

Start by having a little conversation with yourself. Repeat after me, "God made me, and he doesn't make junk. I'm a unique person with lots of ability. I am loved by my Creator . . . and I have the capacity to love—and be loved—by the opposite sex."

You are the Lord's work of art—physically, mentally, and spiritually—but he has given you the responsibility of taking care of his handiwork. Unfortunately, like many other singles—both male and female—you're probably unsure of yourself and wonder where to begin. Hey, that's okay. We all have insecurities. It's up to you—and only you—to face them, then step out in a positive new direction.

Next, take your fears to God. Ask for confidence and for the ability to make your social life great. Then make an effort to meet people, to talk, to listen, and to understand. With God's help, you'll find solutions to your dating problems. And remember: If you're turned down or passed up a few times . . . so what?! Get back on the horse and be persistent . . . and keep praying. That's what I did!

STEP #2: TAKE INVENTORY

Just about everyone, with the possible exception of models, dancers, and professional athletes, could use some improvements. In fact, your whole life works better if your machinery is tuned up. I'm not suggesting that you try to be like the "beautiful people" you see in the movies or plastered on magazine covers. In fact, the opposite is true. You only have to be the best you can be.

It all starts by taking inventory. You might be a little shocked by what I'm about to suggest, but get acquainted with your own physique. Sometime after taking a shower, stand in front of a full-length mirror and evaluate what you see. This is an important step.

As you stand there, don't suck in your gut or put on sunglasses or dim the lights. Study your body as it is. The key is looking at yourself honestly and saying, "This is how God made me . . . and what I see in the mirror is all I have to work with. Is this the best me? Is there room for improvement?"

While examining yourself, keep in mind that your body is the product of both genetics (which you can't alter) and lifestyle (which you can). In fact, your lifestyle can have a profound effect on the visual aspects of genetic makeup: You may have been born with the genes of a decathlon winner, but if your lifestyle has been that of Mr. or Ms. Couch Potato, your body will not appear Olympian.

Mark Finley, a columnist for *Men's Fitness* magazine and a top physical trainer, puts it this way: "You can't work yourself into any body configuration you choose, but every man and woman has many more options than he/she realizes. Inbred limitations can't be totally overcome, but they can definitely be overshadowed: Even the most 'average' person can sculpt a body of choice from his/her particular genetic clay."

STEP #3: DON'T BE A COUCH POTATO

Now comes the hard part: getting off the couch and actually doing something to improve your body. Yes, I'm talking about . . . gulp! . . . exercise.

According to Mark, the trick to a successful shaping-up system is no trick at all. By working out and getting some exercise on a daily basis, you build up your body. And by building up your body, you're dealing in optical illusion. And when you look your best, you feel good too.

"Your body likes to work," Mark says, "God designed it that way. It wants to be strong and fit. If you choose to work out— and get any kind of exercise—you're doing a great thing for yourself. The results will come if you stick with it. That's a fact."

Think about it this way. When your body is flabby, it looks flabby. As you build up your whole body, your whole body looks—and is—less flabby. Moreover, as you continue getting exercise, as your body takes on new dimensions, any physical shortcomings grow less and less evident.

You don't have to make any radical changes or learn to play a smashing game of tennis. What you do have to do is sculpt out the best you from the material at hand—your body and your attitude toward it.

"It's a big mistake to become obsessed with building the perfect body," Mark says. "Your goal shouldn't be to look like Cindy Crawford, Arnold Schwarzenegger, or anyone else. Instead, you want to take what you have and make it the best it can be. And when that's your goal, you'll feel 100-percent better about yourself."

STEP #4: CONNECT WITH CONVERSATION

Once you've jumped into tuning up your attitude and your body, work on your conversations.

Often a single goes on a date or attends a social gathering with an internal alarm going off in their head: *If this person finds out what I'm really like, he/she won't like me at all.*

This kind of self-defeating, automatic inner tape recording is responsible for feelings of shyness, not to mention all kinds of monosyllabic grunts and giggles. So how do you have a meaningful conversation with a man or a woman?

Start by forgetting yourself and turning off that alarm. Make a conscious effort to relax. Don't worry, and don't let unfounded, irrational fears chip away at your self-esteem. Keep telling yourself, "I am not clumsy or stupid, nor am I a hopeless goon who'll spend life as a lonely hermit."

I survived my dating disaster, and I've had fun going out since that unforgettable afternoon. I'm looking forward to successful dates in the future. And like you, I'm determined to end my adventure in singlehood happy . . . whether or not that means marriage.

In case you need a jump start, try these conversation starters:

- *Animals.* People love to talk about their four-legged friends. "Do you have a pet? What's its name? How long have you had it?"

- *Apartments or houses.* It's fun telling how you found your apartment or house, especially if you live in a congested place like Los Angeles or New York.

- *Embarrassing moments.* Be funny and make your date laugh. Pull stuff from the "Twilight Zone Files" of your life. You know . . . like the time you went horseback riding with someone you really, really wanted to impress and ended up getting a grasshopper caught in your pants! (Oh wait . . . that was me. Never mind!)

- *Faith.* Here's a giant area of your life you both have in common (assuming he/she is not part of some strange bull-worshiping, hot-coal-walking cult. But if your friend is, then you shouldn't be romantically interested . . . now should you?!) Talk about what's going on at church, ministries you're involved in . . . neat stuff God is doing in your life.

- *Shopping.* "Where did you get that bracelet? It looks very exotic." Or "I'm shopping for a new CD player. Got any suggestions?"

- *Spare-time activities.* The sky's the limit here. Talk about sports, hobbies, unique excursions you've taken . . . whatever!

- *Vacations.* "Let's say your boss handed you a plane ticket and a month off as a bonus for your hard work. Then he or she looks you in the eye and says, 'We left the ticket blank. Fill it in and go wherever you wish!'

Where would you go? What would you do if money were no obstacle?"

- *Work*. Hey, now you've really hit a topic that's close to home! Unless the person you're interested in is a member of the "Robin Leach Lifestyles of the Rich and Famous Club."

- *You*. But be careful with this topic. If you talk too much about yourself, your date will think you're egotistical. Without bragging or sounding stuck on yourself or telling all your deepest, darkest secrets, fill your date in on what's unique about yourself . . . your hopes, dreams, goals, interests. Remember, be upbeat, honest, and positive.

So get out there . . . and start talking!

CHAPTER 6

How to Meet Potential Dates

Someone once wrote "There is no use waiting for your love boat unless you've sent it out."

This point was illustrated in a college classroom a few years back.

Dr. Leo Buscaglia is a professor at the University of Nevada. He teaches what is called "The Love Class." While I'm unsure if Buscaglia professes a faith in God, he has literally written the book on love—more than a dozen—and has many positive insights on relationships. In his book, *Born for Love*, he tells of a lesson in love his "Love Class" will never forget.

> When I was teaching Love Class, we were once visited by a dog. The dog entered the class fearlessly, wagging its tail and wandering among the seated students, getting all the attention he wanted. The students, of course, responded with pats and caresses, prompting one of the young ladies in the class to observe dryly, "This is so typical of my life. Here I've been hurting all evening with loneliness and not a person has offered me an understanding touch. A stray dog wanders in and is showered with affection! There's something very wrong with that."

"Maybe it's not so crazy," a young man responded. "The dog came in and by his actions told us he was open to loving. His message was simple, nonthreatening and clear. You, on the other hand, just sat there stoically, revealing nothing. We're not mind readers. Sometimes you've just got to speak up or at least give some hints."

———— ·⦁· ————

Visibility is the key. Sitting at home won't do it. Every town, no matter how small, has various organizations and associations. A library. A museum. Music. Athletics. Seminars. Classes. Let everybody—friends and relatives—know you're on a mate-finding journey. Ask for their help.

But the question still remains . . .

WHERE CAN CHRISTIANS LOOK TO FIND A MATE?

If you're like me, you're tired of hearing that worn-out saying, "There are plenty of fish in the sea." I want to know exactly where the fish are biting and exactly how to reel them in. (Actually, I don't enjoy fishing trips, and I'm not out to bag "my limit." I'll be happy with just one, thank you . . . the right one.)

As a committed Christian man, I know where not to look: Singles bars, daily "happy hour" hangouts, cheap weekends in Vegas, cheezy TV "Love Connection"-style game shows . . . forget it! I don't care to be branded with the herds that stampede through those spots. And since I can't dance, disco clubs would spell disaster. Even if I could dance, I wouldn't be caught dead in those places.

After doing a little digging, I learned that creativity is the key. And after talking to all sorts of people—single, married, young, old—I heard the same message: "The sky's the limit. Don't get frustrated . . . get going! We did."

You have four primary waters to cruise—church, work, mutual friends, and recreational hangouts—but within each . . . hey, "the sky's the limit!"

Fountain of Faith

Hands down, the church is the best place to look. Why? The obvious—the chances are good that you'll find a person who shares your values and who's most compatible. And churches offer all sorts of activities, so get involved:

- singles groups
- campouts
- Bible study groups
- service projects
- short-term mission trips
- athletic events

During the summer many church groups host numerous activities: baseball, volleyball, picnics, and retreats. Don't be pushy or attend these events like a wolf hunting for its next "kill." At the church I belong to, I know of a woman who attends functions like these, scouting out "new prey." She'll walk up to guys she's never met before, stick out her hand and say, "Hi! I'm single. Are you? (True story. I'm not kidding!)

The key: Go to the activities you feel comfortable attending, be visible, and be yourself. Never look desperate. Do your best to meet people, then leave the rest in God's hands.

The Workplace

I know what you're thinking. Come on, Mike, it's bad news to date someone at the office.

Yes, I've heard the warnings, but I disagree. Here's why.

First, while some companies frown on office romances—even to the extent that if two people in the company marry, one must leave—my reaction is, "Isn't it better to find love and change jobs?" Of course, if your dream job is at stake, then you have some serious soul-searching to do. Bottom line: Set your priorities. What's most important to you?

Also, it's a natural place where lots of people gather with a common goal. At the workplace you not only get to know a lot of people, but you also have something in common with others around you.

If you work in a large organization, your chances of finding romance are increased. Big corporations have many employee activities—yearly picnics, staff meetings, seminars, extracurricular courses, a company cafeteria or lunchroom. These are all excellent places to meet others, and you have a built-in topic of conversation. It's not too hard to plunk your lunch tray down by a fellow employee and begin talking.

Healthy Hangouts

If you're active in sports or hobbies, checking out the recreation scene is an ideal place to find a mate. But beware. It can also be hazardous to your health and reputation. Let me explain.

A few years back in an effort to make some friends—and maybe land a date—I attended a volleyball party hosted by my church's singles group. It was my first appearance at a singles' event, so I wanted to make a good impression.

The game got under way, and I was doing pretty well— especially on the friendship front. That is, until the other team got ahead. Then I transformed into Mr. Win-at-All-Costs and became a serious court hog. And that's when it happened.

A female teammate and I went for the volleyball at the same time. Wham!

I not only made contact with the ball, I also nailed her face. She buckled over and began to moan. When she looked up ... ouch! ... blood was streaming from her nose. Half the singles group, obviously all her friends, rushed to her aid.

I just stood on the court mumbling, "Please believe me, I don't always play this way. And I'm not some twisted abuser. I'm sorry. Really."

I would have given anything to melt through the tiny cracks on the floor. Great, just great, I thought. I really made a cool impression on this crowd.

Moral of the story: Don't get so caught up in the game that you lose perspective. And remember why you're on the court (to win a date, of course).

With this in mind, let's check out the recreation rapids.

- *Health clubs:* Even among non-Christians, this has become the modern meeting place for singles. Something to do with the current health craze. So, whether you need it or not (and most of us need it), consider a membership in a health or fitness club.
- *Sporting events:* This offers a mixed bag of possibilities. Basketball, hockey, and softball are good bets for singles looking for other singles. Tennis matches, sailing events, and swim meets are other possibilities.
- *Craft fairs:* Craftspeople come from near and far to sell their wares, and that means a large gathering of people.
- *Clubs:* Do you like to hike? There are plenty of groups—some just for singles—that take regular trips. Enjoy exploring caves? Maybe you're the type who's into high-adventure whitewater rafting trips through, say, the Grand Canyon. Let your fingers do the walking through the Yellow Pages, and learn about clubs in your area. Give them a call, and ask if they have special events just for singles.

Pool of Possibilities: A Checklist of Where to Look

- competitions
- art galleries (especially openings)
- cooking classes
- photography clubs
- concerts in the park
- friends, relatives
- theater groups
- dog/cat shows
- political conventions
- trade shows
- local science groups
- nature/backpacking clubs

Friendship Connection

My friend Pam found success through her pool of friends. Here's her story:

> Friends are a big help. My relationship with the guy I'm dating now all came about in a weird way. Basically, he saw my picture on a poster at church. He approached one of the pastors, a very close friend of mine, and asked, "Who is this lady?"
>
> The pastor responded, "Oh, you guys have to meet!"
>
> The whole matchmaker thing happened. The pastor filled me in about this guy . . . and I ended up taking his advice. If my friend recommended this guy, then I knew he must be pretty solid. We talked on the phone for three months before we ever met each other. And when we started dating, I was happy I was introduced to him.

I suggest you tap into your circle of friends. They can be the best help in finding the right person to date. Why? If your friendship is close, then they know you—as well as the kind of person you'd be interested in. They can also help you avoid getting into a miserable situation.

Love at First Byte?

If you have access to a computer and a modem, you're all set to cruise cyberspace . . . and with a little patience, you can even land a date. That's exactly how it happened for Jim, a thirty-seven-year-old aerospace worker in southern California.

"One day my buddy logged on to a romance connection on America Online, then entered a 'chat room,'" Jim says. "Before I knew it, I was communicating with Judy—a twenty-six-year-old Christian woman who doesn't live in my area.

"In the weeks that followed, I ended up making contact with Judy from my own computer at home. Soon we began to E-mail each other, and eventually we decided it was time for an F2F (face-to-face) encounter."

Jim and Judy agreed to meet each other one evening at Disneyland. Their first date was a hit. They made plans for

---

Time reports that there are a hundred thousand haunts online—each with its own crowd, own interests and own point of view. Here are a few:

- Singles. Currently, the hottest pickup spots are chat rooms of America Online's People Connection.
- Christians. *Christianity Today* offers two chat rooms on America Online: Fellowship Hall 1 and 2.
- Twentysomething Gen-Xers hang at Manhattan's MindVox and contemplate fifty more years of living under the shadow of Yuppies.

their next outing, then their next. At press time, the two are still seeing each other.

"Meeting people in cyberspace is the best way to go," Jim says. "As a Christian, I'm not into the singles bar scene. And I can maintain my privacy through the Internet."

But beware. On the flip side, relationships can be complicated in cyberspace. The very technology that draws most people together also keeps them apart. Like Jim, you can live in California and strike up a friendship with someone in New York.

Also, you can't always trust that the person on the other end of the line is, in fact, who he or she claims to be. An article in *Time* reports that most net users are more likely to project aspects of the person they wish they could be. In other words, you may think you're talking to a twenty-six-year-old Christian single from southern California, but she may be a lonely thirteen-year-old teenager from the Midwest.

Popular Online Services

- America Online
- Prodigy
- CompuServe
- Internet

"Judy and I held off meeting each other until we felt comfortable with each other," Jim says. "We also made sure that the person on the other end was telling the truth. That's what I recommend to other online users."

Meeting potential dates can be tricky and risky. Friends, the Internet, church, work, and recreational activities are the best sources for finding potential dates. So, get going on your search!

CHAPTER 7

Creating Safeguards

I was a youth minister for seven years after college graduation. Never once did I worry about anyone reading something in to my giving one of the teen guys a ride home after an activity.

That was several years ago. Things have changed . . . or maybe I just had it a little easier because I'm female.. I have male friends in youth ministry who have to be much more careful. It seems too easy nowadays for someone to start a rumor or create something calculated out of innocence.

Lewis, a youth minister friend of mine, shared his standards with me. "When I'm taking kids home from a church activity, I never take a girl home last," he said, "unless she has a girlfriend with her." And if she didn't have a girlfriend with her? He'd drop her off at another teen's home and ask her to call for someone to come get her while he waited.

Lewis was careful to create wonderful safeguards. This carried over to his office hours and what he practiced in the church. "When a teen girl calls and wants to stop by the office for counseling," he told me, "I let her know ahead of time that my door will always be partially open while she's here. I want people to know I'm in my office with a female. No secrets. Nothing to hide."

And if she has to talk about something really personal and doesn't want the secretary within hearing range? "I advise her to bring a close, trusted friend. That's the only way I'll shut the door," he said.

I appreciate that. A godly man who loves his wife and kids enough to create safeguards. It's not always easy to build hedges. But as singles, it's important that we do.

Again, in my days of youth ministry, things were a little different. One particular memory stands out: I had been asked to speak at a church camp two hours from where I lived. I accepted the invitation on one condition: Instead of concluding the camp on Friday morning, I would give my final message on Thursday evening. The reason? I was taking my own youth group on a two-week choir tour from Oklahoma City to southern California, and we were scheduled to depart at 5:30 Friday morning.

The Thursday evening service would begin at 7:00 with all the preliminaries, such as singing, announcements, awards, testimonies, and so forth. I wouldn't actually get up to speak until close to 8:00. Then after I spent some time praying with teens after the service, I wouldn't be able to pull away till 9:30 or 10:00. I would not arrive back home until close to midnight.

Several people suggested I take one of the teen guys from my own youth group. My mom said, "We'd just feel better knowing you'll have a guy with you—in case you have a flat tire or something. After all, it'll be so late."

So I asked Brad, one of our high school sophomores who also sang, to accompany me on the trip and provide a special song during the service. He was ecstatic. His parents were thrilled. And we had a terrific time. Never once did anyone question my taking a teen guy on a two-hour late night trip alone. Everyone wanted me to take a male.

Things have changed, haven't they? Because of inappropriate advances and even full-fledged affairs, we've had to start building hedges. It's sad that we've lost some of our innocence—but wise that we're striving to be as careful as possible to avoid even the appearance of something that could be construed as sinful.

Again, as singles, we're prime targets for having holes in our hedges. We can't be too careful. It only takes one teen girl, who has a crush on her youth minister, to make one false statement ("Barry likes me. I mean really likes me. He looks at me in a special way.") to ruin a person's career. Even if there's no truth to the statement at all, that person's character will undoubtedly be under question.

THE ANSWER: CREATING SAFEGUARDS

So what's the solution? Make time to create solid safeguards. Here are my suggestions for some specific rules:

Rule #1: Wear the Word. If you travel, carry your Bible with you as a constant reminder of God's expectations.

Rule #2: Monitor motels. Realize that motels are filled with choices. Let's say you're finished with your meeting and head back to your room only to realize you're thirsty. The bar is still open. Do you go there for a Coke or do you grab one from the machine?

You're alone and bored. Stretched out on the king-sized bed, you begin flipping through the channels. Practically every motel has pay TV. Do you keep flipping or compromise—settling for something a godly man or woman should avoid?

A good-looking member of the opposite sex approaches you. Again, you're lonely. No one will know if you have a little fun. You've already determined not to have sex . . . but why not enjoy some heated, physical passion?

Rule #3: Protect your prayers. You're very involved in your church. Your pastor is a dynamic, polished speaker. Several times you've felt the presence of God as people have gone forward to pray. You find yourself kneeling close to and praying with members of the opposite sex. Examine your motives. Is it because you really care about their spiritual condition? Or because it feels good to be hugged and touched during an emotional moment?

Rule #4: Acquire accountability. It's much easier to create and maintain safeguards if someone knows what you're doing. Consider allowing someone whom you trust spiritually to hold you accountable in the weak or questionable areas of your life.

Scott and Rick, both in editing and publishing, meet twice a month to maintain a level of accountability to each other. Both have careers that involve travel. They have developed a deep, intimate level of trust with one another and have unspoken permission to ask anything. "When Rick returns home from being on the road, I know exactly what to ask him," Scott says. "I know what's going on in his mind as he sits alone in a motel room. I know because he's told me. He's made himself accountable to me."

Likewise, Scott has revealed his vulnerable areas to Rick. By developing such a deep level of spiritual intimacy with each other, they have, in essence, created some wonderful safeguards which protect not only them but their families as well.

Singles need this kind of accountability even more. Because of the freedom that comes with singlehood, we have the option of pulling up and heading out any weekend we want. Whether it's to visit family, camp out, take a trip with friends, or explore the mountains, we're not tied down. When something exciting beckons, we have the freedom to go.

Therefore, it can be easy to miss church. Will anyone really check up on us if we're not there? *Oh, she's probably out of town again,* they'll think. Because of my heavy speaking schedule, I travel quite a bit. I want someone to know where I am when I'm not at church. That's why I've given my prayer partner my speaking schedule. I don't ever want it to become easy to miss church. I know if I'm not scheduled to be out of town, I'd better be at church! She's going to call me on it if I'm not.

I've also given her a list of questions to ask me when I return from a speaking engagement. Again, I know someone is going to hold me accountable for my time away from home. What did I do in my free time? Did I minister effectively? What kind of attitude did I have? All this helps me create effective safeguards.

Are you willing to invest the time needed to find an accountability partner? It'll take a lot of prayer on your part—seeking God's direction about whom you should approach. And it'll require effort: building trust, making yourself vulnerable, maybe even listing your weak areas and giving them to this person so he/she can ask you about them on a regular basis.

Why not come up with some rules for yourself—standards that you refuse to compromise?

We've talked about a variety of safeguards. But let's get specific now and focus on how we as singles can create hedges with married people. Married people can seem safe because they're married, but it's all too easy to fall into an undesirable relationship with a married person without planning to. Here's what can happen:

IT ALWAYS HURTS!

Take Jenna and Todd, for example. Even though both were married, their rationalization is common among many singles. Both had emotional needs that were not being met by their spouses.

Jenna was young, beautiful, and employed in a brand-new local day-care center. Todd was the young, handsome, newly hired day-care director who had just completed his M.B.A.

He had dreamed that this day-care center would be something he and his wife would do together. Even though the main responsibility was his, he assumed his wife would help and support him in doing all she could to help it grow into a successful business.

But his wife was busy trying to get the new house in order and keeping up with their two preschool boys. She had little energy to contribute to Todd's ideas for promotions and growth of the center, and she reminded him when he tried to recruit her help that their family came first.

So he began to look elsewhere for help. He began to focus on Jenna. Since she worked in the office, she was already involved to some degree in the growing business—typing newsletters, helping him organize details, and so forth. At his invitation, she agreed to become involved in a special promotional campaign that involved some after-hours work.

During office hours, their discussions centered on problems with the center's children, ideas for workable solutions, and future plans for the center. Through their common interests and concern in building a solid program, their own friendship began to grow. Jenna found it easy to talk with Todd ... and he was all ears! Since her own husband came home tired—from working construction and investing his evening hours in real estate classes—he didn't really have the energy to be as attentive to her needs as she wanted him to be.

And when Todd got home? His wife was still questioning their move to this town. She was also lonely because she hadn't made friends, and she was frustrated with Todd because he spent so much time at the center. The result? His home wasn't a haven he could return to each day—it was a place of stress and tension. He found himself staying at the office later and later.

And Jenna? It was easy to rationalize that Todd needed her help—after all, she was the secretary. Wasn't it her responsibility to help him create the best day-care program possible?

It became convenient for both to work after everyone else in the office had gone home. And they both had to eat, so it seemed natural that Todd would order a pizza or treat Jenna to a burger at a place close-by. You can guess what happened.

As they spent more time together, developing an emotional bond of intimacy that should have been reserved for their spouses, they found themselves attracted to one another. Both discussed the marital difficulties in their own homes, needs that weren't being met, and one thing led to another.

You can imagine the hurt that the two families experienced because of the affair. And it all started because two people didn't take the time to create safeguards.

As singles, we're even more vulnerable! So how can we protect ourselves from these situations and behaviors?

SAFEGUARDS WITH MARRIED PEOPLE

Rule #1: Don't go out to eat alone with a member of the opposite sex who's married. Again, we all have a need to become emotionally intimate with someone. A married person is outside your boundary. Don't set yourself up. Are we saying you can't be friends with someone of the opposite sex who's married? Well . . . no. But make wise decisions. Become friends with his/her spouse as well, and avoid time spent alone with your married friend.

Rule #2: Don't go fishing for compliments from a married member of the opposite sex. "How do you think this dress looks on me?" "Do you like this sweater?" You're striving to have your emotional needs met—which is natural—but be selective about whom you ask to meet those needs. Again, an opposite sex married friend is out of your boundary.

Rule #3: Don't listen to a member of the opposite sex tell you his/her marriage troubles. They need to talk. But as a single person, you're out of their boundaries. Encourage them to share problems with their spouse. There's nothing you can do to help anyway, besides listening. As a result of the sharing process, you'll begin to develop an emotional attachment with this person. It's natural. Whenever we share with anyone, a bond is created.

Rule #4: Beware of any chemistry between you and a married member of the opposite sex. Be honest with yourself. Don't rationalize. This is where an accountability partner can really help. If you are feeling some electricity between yourself and a married friend at work, tell your prayer partner! Now is the time to be praying about your feelings, your strategy for change, and your decision to build hedges.

AND IF WE DON'T BUILD HEDGES?

When we refuse to make the time to create effective safeguards, we fall into a dangerous trap of rationalizing. So if you're not building some protective hedges around your life, ask yourself why. It could be because of two things:

You're trying to fill an emotional hole. Often, we singles fail to create solid hedges because we're trying to meet an emotional need. Everyone has an inborn need to relate to someone on an emotionally intimate level. When those needs aren't met in our immediate circle of friends, it's easy to rationalize and search for others outside our boundaries who will meet those needs.

Laziness. Face it: Building hedges takes energy and commitment. It's much easier to sit back and think: *I know what my weaknesses are. Nothing's going to happen.* Think of it this way: By creating some healthy safeguards now, you're actually investing in your future. You're establishing a necessary, godly discipline to your life that will reflect in your relationship with your future spouse and family. Instead of waiting until marriage to build hedges, start creating those boundaries now. Then if you marry, it'll be much easier to maintain what you've already established.

BOTTOM LINE

It all comes down to wanting to be all God needs us to be, doesn't it? It's certainly a lot easier not to be careful! But as singles who want to live fulfilling lives without regrets, it just makes sense to create some safeguards.

Mike and I are both editors for Focus on the Family. We work for a company that has some strict policies for members of the opposite sex. For instance, we can't fly anywhere together alone. If we are out of town together at a convention, seminars or other event, we're not allowed to have dinner together alone.

That may sound harsh, but I'm grateful for a company that is out to protect me. Think about it. We're overprotective of those we love, aren't we? I feel privileged to work for an employer who loves me enough to help create some hedges that I may have overlooked.

We'd much rather be too careful than live with regret.

CHAPTER 8

Brokenhearted: How to Survive Breakup

I slapped off the alarm and squinted at the clock. It was 4:30 A.M. The weekend. My day off. I rolled over and buried my head in the pillow.

Life doesn't begin at this hour, I told myself.

Then a face appeared in my mind: Sherry. I quickly remembered my whole reason for interrupting a perfectly good slumber and bolted out of bed. But as I twisted on the shower faucet and adjusted the water, a jabbing pain shot through my stomach. Suddenly, my emotions took a nosedive.

Today was our big date, yet I felt miserable. Last week, I couldn't wait to see her again. This week was a different story. Why?

Sherry and I had been dating for nearly a month. But the problem was that we had a long-distance relationship. She lives in Santa Fe. My home is in Colorado Springs. We also have an age difference. I am nine years older. But we both stayed in touch and determined to make our relationship work.

"Next Saturday, I'll leave the house by 5:30 A.M. and get to your place by 12:00," I had told her. The date was set. We had planned a nonstop blast in Santa Fe.

Yet I couldn't help feeling that something was wrong. Her voice sounded distant. She didn't laugh as usual. And the last letter she wrote was signed "Sherry." That was it. No "Love, Sher" or "I miss you."

I felt her pulling away.

"Why?" I prayed as I zoomed down I–25. "She's incredible, and we have so much in common. God, I love her. I want her to be my wife. I want the search to be over . . . please."

As I neared the New Mexico border, I found myself slowing the car. I knew what was ahead: The end of our relationship.

During dinner that night, it happened.

"You're the best guy I've ever dated," she started. "But let's just stick with friendship."

I gulped some water and crunched the ice. My face must have turned ten shades of red. Then I said the most stupid thing possible, "What a relief. I was thinking the exact same thing. Wow, it feels as though a giant burden has been lifted."

I sat back in my chair and sulked inside. *How could this have happened? Was God playing some kind of sick joke? Would I ever find the right woman?*

What He Felt
- Hurt
- Insecurity
- Shock
- Embarrassment
- Confusion
- Anger
- Fear
- Depression

What She Felt
- Fear
- Uncertainty
- Confusion
- Insecurity
- Crowded
- Dread
- Pressure
- Relief

BREAKING UP: A DEFINITION

As you can see, breaking up amounts to one very painful, very lonely, almost-worse-than-death-and-avoid-at-any-cost experience: Rejection!

And it seems as though we've all been programmed since childhood to avoid rejection. After all, take a look at a dictionary's definition of *reject*: "To discard or throw out as worthless, useless, or substandard; to rebuff, deny acceptance, care, and love to someone."

We all know what it feels like to be rejected. But when you're the one doing the rejecting, it sometimes doesn't feel as bad. It often feels good. Why? It's actually pretty complicated to understand since each situation is different. But in most cases, it's a matter of power. What we said or did controlled another person's feelings. It somehow made us feel powerful, like we were in charge and called the shots.

It's also safe.

I could have told myself that I know Sherry is unhappy with this relationship, and there's a good chance she might break up with me. I think I'll beat her to it and save us both from a lot of trouble.

In truth, this would have saved me from a lot of pain—and kept my pride from being bruised. But I know that dating involves risk. Each time I get into a relationship, I'm making myself vulnerable to another person. I'm actually putting my heart and emotions on the line. And the bottom line is that the dating relationship will move in one of two directions: marriage or breakup.

IS CUPID STUPID? (TIPS ON HANDLING BREAKUP)

Keep in mind an important distinction: Dating does not equal marriage. It's part of the process of finding a marriage partner. The right partner.

You're searching for a person with whom you'll spend the rest of your life. And that's a long time—especially if the man or woman whom you think you can't live without truly isn't the right fit.

After a short time of dating Sherry, here's what I wrote in my journal:

God, I'm in love with her. She's exactly the kind of woman I want to marry. We have so much in common. I love being with her and can't imagine spending another day without someone like her. Thank you for putting Sherry in my life. Please let my search be over. Let her be the one.

But as I began to look back over my journal, two phrases jumped out at me: "the kind of woman" and "someone like her." The truth is that Sherry is the type of partner I am looking for, but she wasn't necessarily the woman of my life. And I wrote this in my journal after only one week of knowing her. In fact, I was infatuated with a type. I really didn't have enough information to know for sure if she was the woman for me.

WHAT I'VE LEARNED

Believe it or not, a breakup can turn out okay, and life does go on. In fact, future dating can be tons of fun and a lot less painful once we understand a few things.

Prayer. From the start of a relationship, commit Isaiah 22:22 to prayer and apply it to your circumstances: "I will place on his shoulder the key to the house of David; what he opens no one can shut, and what he shuts no one can open."

Ask God for wisdom every step of the way, during good times and bad. And trust that he has your best interests in mind.

Honesty. One of the most hurtful things you can do in a relationship is to play head games with your dating partner. Leading him or her to believe you have deeper feelings than you do can be devastating. And most of us are such pros at playing games, many times we don't even realize we're doing it.

For instance, writing "I love you" notes just because it feels good at the time (perhaps you're in an especially good mood) and calling constantly all communicate one thing: "I'm crazy about you, and I'm committed to you." But if your heart doesn't match your actions, you're playing a brutal head game.

Careful with the "L" word. Separate infatuation from true love, and don't be too quick to throw around this four-letter word. In fact, it's a good idea to never casually throw it around—especially when it comes to a dating relationship.

Again, be honest. Don't shower someone with tons of attention if you're insecure about the relationship. Share what you're feeling and let your actions reflect caution.

Communication. Learn the art of good conversation skills. Ask questions of your date that go beyond yes/no answers. This enables you to learn more about the person on the inside and lets them know you care.

Too often, we'll find dates who are such good listeners or very happy just to be dating that they'll gladly do all the receiving—listening to us for hours so that we end up neglecting them and not really getting to know much about them.

Soul-searching. Don't be afraid to ask yourself—and your dating partner—some hard questions: Can I live without this person? Why do I believe he/she is God's best for me? Why do I believe I should be married? Could I handle the possibility of a lifetime of singleness? What are my real motives for being in this relationship?

FACING THE FUTURE

Do some soul-searching and then wrestle with reality:

This person may not be the best choice. Yes, life will go on. I can survive this breakup, and I can live without him/her. God understands my pain and cares deeply about my desires. He will help me through this.

Don't be in so much of a hurry to get married that you latch on to anyone who shows serious interest. Take your time getting to know him or her. If you don't, you might find yourself not liking your new love interest when you get to know him or her better. That means having to break up, and as the song says, "Breaking up is hard to do." So try to avoid getting into that situation as much as possible.

Also consider what popular author Tim Stafford has said about singleness:

> One of the saddest things I see is the tendency for single people to live life as though waiting for something or someone to happen to them. They act as though they are in limbo, waiting to become capable of life when the magic day at the altar comes. Of course, they're usually disappointed. In some cases they become such poor specimens of humanity that no one wants to marry them. More often they do get married only to discover that they haven't received the key to life: the initiative and character they should have developed before marriage is exactly what they need in marriage. And they are still left lonely and frustrated.

CHAPTER 9

Breaking Hearts: How to Break Up Without a Black Eye

Being on the receiving end of a breakup is brutal, but it's no less easy when you have to do the rejecting.

Not long before my relationship with Sherry, I dated a woman named Ashley. We had gone out a month and enjoyed each other's company, but I knew in my heart a long-term relationship—let alone marriage—just wasn't in the picture. For me, friendship hadn't turned into romantic love. For Ashley, it was an entirely different matter.

Cupid had struck and she was head over heels in love. And our married friends at church seemed to fuel the flames. We received all kinds of well-meaning advice:

"You're a perfect match! The two of you have so much in common ... how could your relationship not be God's will?!"

"Don't expect perfection in your mate. Remember, love is blind. My advice: Take the plunge!"

"You kids aren't getting any younger. So you'd better ... you know ... set the date."

Our relationship was cruising full speed ahead, and I knew what I had to do: Break up ... immediately. But how?

Hurting her was the last thing I wanted to do. Night after night, I'd wrestle with a flood of confusing thoughts and emotions: She's great, and she'd be a wonderful wife for some lucky man. Why am I not in love with her? Why does she want more than just friendship? How can I share my true feelings with her without hurting her?

So I ended up doing the wrong thing: I tried to taper off from our relationship instead of severing the ties completely. I broke a few dates and made some excuses from time to time, but I continued seeing her.

Maybe she'll catch on, I reasoned with myself. If I act cold from time to time and break a few dates, maybe she'll catch on.

"Ashley, I'm really tired tonight. Let's not get together tonight," became my standard line. Big mistake.

Ashley never caught on. She wasn't a mind reader. Instead, I ended up sending her the wrong messages. I even gave her hope for our future together. And just as I had avoided what I had to do, she completely blocked from her mind any possibility of breakup.

We eventually severed our ties, but at the expense of much emotional damage to both of us. This whole episode made me realize how little I knew about the opposite sex . . . or this crazy thing called love. I especially had a lot to learn about relating to the opposite sex, not to mention a thing or two about honesty. Every mistake I wanted to avoid I ended up making.

Perhaps you can identify with what I felt—whether you've experienced the brunt of a breakup or faced the difficult decision to call off a relationship you've been in. Here's what I learned. Maybe it will help you avoid the mistakes I made.

HOW TO BREAK UP: DO'S AND DON'TS

Do find a private place. Getting away from people is a must because privacy is very important during an emotional experience like this. You may think a restaurant is a safer and more appropriate place to end a relationship, but in reality you're actually dropping a bomb. So provide a place in which your partner can explode: tears, screaming, frustration. And the fact is, none of this can happen in a restaurant.

Do express your feelings with sensitivity. Take a deep breath and face the issue. Calmly talk through your decision and why you think it would be better to separate. "We don't have anything in common." "All we do is fight." "You hurt me when you . . ." Just get right to the point and share what's on your heart. Never say things like, "Let's just be friends!" You're not in junior high anymore.

Have courage and face the difficult task head on. A coward never really explains his or her true feelings. That's exactly how I acted . . . like a coward.

Don't get into a heated finger-pointing match. Expressing your emotions is one matter but seeking to prove that your date is an "insensitive mass of refuse who's using up Earth's precious oxygen" really won't solve a thing. While it may be true, you'll both end up walking away with a lot of extra hurt. And if you don't deal with that hurt, you could end up with some deep scars—which could affect your next relationship.

Do wait for his/her response. And listen carefully to the other person's opinions. Remember, just because you want to break up doesn't mean this person has in fact suddenly transformed into an "insensitive mass of refuse" that you must quickly throw out.

Don't get defensive. Your friend may not agree with what you've said and end up treating you like a repulsive mole. Make every effort to deflate the tension—don't give in to it.

WHEN YOU END A RELATIONSHIP . . .

As you work through a difficult thing like breakup, stick to the reasons why you believe it's the best choice. Hold it up in prayer.

And if the person you're breaking up with tries to talk you out of your decision, stick to your guns. The last thing you want or need is to stay in a relationship with someone you really don't want to be with. That could lead to even deeper hurt.

It would be ridiculous to keep a scorecard on everyone we meet, looking for the perfect person. There's just no such thing as a perfect person. But it is important to set your standards high and enter a relationship carefully.

Take a look at these Scripture verses. What do they tell you about marriage and singleness? Do they reinforce your decision to break up?

- 1 Corinthians 7:7–9
- 1 Corinthians 7:32–35
- Matthew 6:33; 19:22

Remember to pray about the situation, asking God to help you say the right words. You don't want to hurt the other person in your haste to get out of an undesirable or uncomfortable relationship. Remember, that person is God's child, too, and God wants what's best for both of you.

PART THREE:

Understanding the Opposite Sex

CHAPTER 10

Basic Major Differences Between Men and Women

Not all women are emotional time bombs just waiting to explode, nor is every man an insensitive Neanderthal. But that's how we're often portrayed on TV. Check out our zany descriptions. While some stem from a silly commercial mentality, others are true . . . and a few just might hit home.

Women want to get close to men.	Men want to get close to women who will leave them alone.
Women tend to join in the congregational singing at church.	Men tend to laugh at the women singing.
Women enjoy 480-page romance novels.	Men enjoy TV and a 480-channel remote.
Women aren't afraid to cry during sad movies.	Men choke back the tears or say something like, "Oh, I . . . ah . . . just got something caught in my eye."
Women worry about waistlines.	Men worry about waistlines and hairlines.

Women can talk for hours about anything.	Men stick to the facts, ma'am.
Women buy cute cars in cool colors.	Men buy cool cars with tough engines.
Women pretend they aren't hungry at office parties and eat later.	Men rush the line, eat everything they can get their hands on, and fill paper towels from the bathroom with leftovers so they won't have to make dinner.
Women want a protector.	Men want to protect.
Women linger in a tub full of bubbles.	Men prefer quick showers and a shave.
Women like board games.	Men get bored at games.
Women love long walks through the country.	Men love fast cars on country roads.
Women prefer men who stand up for what they believe.	Men prefer women who believe in what they stand up for.

BUT SERIOUSLY ...

There are a few more differences we can talk about. Willard Harley, in his book *His Needs, Her Needs,* lists the five most basic needs, in order of their importance, of married men and women.

For Men:

1. Sexual fulfillment
2. Recreational companionship
3. An attractive spouse
4. Domestic support
5. Admiration

For Women:

1. Affection
2. Conversation
3. Honesty and openness
4. Financial support
5. Family commitment

That's quite a difference, isn't it! Even though Dr. Harley is speaking about married couples, most of these needs apply to single men and women as well. It just makes sense then—considering the differences between males and females—that a successful relationship will take time, work, and commitment.

AND THAT'S NOT ALL!

Guys are also more fact oriented while women are generally emotion driven. Of course, there are exceptions. But on the whole, women are concerned about discussing and sharing emotionally while men want the quick details so they can get on to something else.

SEXUAL FULFILLMENT: HIS FIRST NEED

Let's just be blunt about it: Outside of marriage it's a sin. It'll always be a sin. For the Christian? No option. No compromises. Nothing we can rationalize about it.

Much of the temptation to succumb to sexual pressure comes from a lack of sexual boundaries. It's frightening to realize that many single adults have never set realistic physical boundaries with the opposite sex. Many are committed to remaining a virgin until marriage but have never thought long and hard about exactly where to draw the line physically. In other words, how far is too far?

If we're still asking this question as an adult, it's obvious that we need to do some immediate soul-searching. Many single adults are confusing virginity with sexual purity. But the truth of the matter is that although one may technically be a virgin on his wedding night, he may not necessarily be sexually pure.

Sexual purity is much more than refraining from the act of intercourse—it involves our entire lifestyle. It's allowing the

Holy Spirit to govern every single area of our lives and accepting his power to help us live above sexual temptation—whether it be in person, on screen, or inside the pages of a book or magazine. (Flip to chapter 17 for a more thorough discussion of sexual purity.)

Commitment to Purity

Be willing to appear "too straight" if necessary to keep and maintain your sexual purity.

- Share your commitment with a trusted same-sex Christian friend. Let someone know exactly where you stand with physical affection.
- Make a list of areas of sexual vulnerability (the HBO channel, being alone and away from home, etc.) and give that list to your trusted same-sex Christian friend (or accountability partner). Allow him/her to quiz you—at unexpected times—on how you're doing in each area.
- Call on the power and strength of the Holy Spirit to keep you from compromising your sexual commitment.

AFFECTION: HER FIRST NEED

Guys, since she wants affection, please take time to reach for her hand, open doors, send cards. These are all signs of affection—which to a woman tells her your mind is on making her feel special. That goes a looong way with us! Know why? Because affection from her dating partner helps bond the relationship. To a woman, it means security—and yes—even a mild form of commitment.

LET'S HAVE FUN!

Notice the number two need of men—recreational companionship. And the number two need of women? Conversation! While her dating companion is out playing a game of touch football or shooting hoops, she's on the phone talking about how she feels about his being gone!

Every good relationship is built on a foundation of commonality. This doesn't mean you're just alike; it does mean you share at least a few similar interests. Since the number two need of males is recreational companionship, strive to find an activity that you and your partner can enjoy together.

You're not athletic? Doesn't matter. Recreation isn't always a rugged sport. Here are a few suggestions we have come up with:

Simplistic Recreation

- Learn to play horseshoes.
- Develop an ongoing board-game tourney with each other. At the end of every three weeks, the one who's behind in the total scoring treats the other to dinner.
- Hiking. (What? There are no trails in your area? Forge a regular path in the mall.)
- Go swimming at the health club or a nearby lake. Or kick back in a Jacuzzi and melt away the stress.
- Head for the local bowling alley. And don't worry about how you look or perform. Just have fun!
- Garden together.
- Hunt for leaves or rocks.
- Purchase a disposable camera (you can get them in the film department at most grocery stores) and head off on a photo safari. You could probably spend an entire day in the park taking crazy pictures of one another.

WOMEN WANT TO TRUST MEN

A female wants to bond or cement her relationships. Her closest female friendships are built around trust—which is created through openness and sharing. This isn't natural for most men. They don't necessarily want to sit around and share how they feel. They want to get close to a woman who will leave them alone!

While it's important for guys to learn how to effectively express their thoughts and feelings, it's likewise important for women not to nag and constantly analyze a man's every action. If he's quiet one evening, it doesn't necessarily mean he's put up a wall. Maybe he simply had a rough day at work and is still contemplating a solution to an office problem.

GETTING HIM TO TALK

Instead of barraging him with a million questions about his day, his current problems, or his lack of openness, ask him questions instead that will be fun to answer and still require some thought and openness. Vulnerability requires practice, patience, and persistence. Here are a few fun starters.

- If you could create the perfect "dream date," what would it be?
- Describe your life if you would have been born in the early 1800s.
- What's the first question you'll ask God when you're in heaven?
- If you were guaranteed your book would be published, what would you write about, and what would the title be?
- Describe the last time you laughed hysterically.
- If you could make a guest appearance on any TV show (past or present), what character would you play and what show would you appear on?

ADMIRATION

While every man needs to be admired by the special woman in his life, fake admiration is easily spotted. Don't pretend to admire something you really don't. And likewise, strive to refrain from dishing out compliments without taking the time to think them through.

Make a mental list of specific things you admire about the special person in your life and focus on complimenting those areas. Chances are he/she will not only respond with gratitude but will work even harder at enhancing what you admire the most.

Creative Admiration

- Janet delivered a bag of candy malted Easter eggs to Will with a note that read, "Glad you're a part of my life. I admire your ability to 'hop to it' in areas of leadership and responsibility."
- When Ronnie treated Mindy to a special Fourth of July picnic, she presented him with a dozen sparklers and told him how much she admired his creativity in planning their dates.
- Gwen mailed three two-dollar bills (yes, you can still get them at the bank if you ask for them!) to Brian at his motel when he had to be out of town on business for three weeks. The message? "I've missed having lunch with you. I love the way you make me feel when you treat me to fun little surprise lunches at McDonald's, The Ice Cream Shoppe, or our favorite pancake house. Here's six. Have lunch on me this time."

Remember that men and women are different. They have different needs and perceive situations differently. Both sexes need to be aware of that so feelings don't get hurt and expectations aren't placed on either sex without thinking. Men need to learn to communicate their feelings and thoughts, and women need to understand that men do think differently than they do. That's what makes life interesting—and challenging.

CHAPTER 11

She Said That, But He Heard This

All evening, Bob had trouble communicating with Connie. Now he'd reached his breaking point. *What is with this woman?* he wondered. *Why is she acting like "Miss Ice Queen"? What does she want from me?*

Around them, the restaurant was filled with the usual buzz of conversation, clinking silverware, and mouthwatering aromas. But the couple sat at opposite ends of a table, Connie toying with her chicken salad and Bob munching his barbecue ribs. He replayed the evening in his mind.

I picked her up at her house and whisked her off to what I was sure would be a knockout evening at our favorite dinner spot. In the car I told her all about my day and she . . . Hmmm, she didn't say a word. Then, when I opened the door to the restaurant, and commented about how I love coming here with her, that's when she slugged me between the eyes with that stinging comment, "Are you sure you mean me . . . or were you thinking of one of your past girlfriends?"

Bob took a sip of water, then cleared his throat. *Got to defuse this bomb.* "Uh, look, hon—out the window. Isn't that the most beautiful blue sky you've ever seen?"

"It's okay. But clouds are rolling in. It'll rain soon. It always does."

Okay, try the "feely" stuff. "Uh, bad day at the office, honey?"

Connie just glared at him.

Bob locked eyes with her. "'Fess up, Con. What's wrong with you? Why are you acting this way?"

That's when she unloaded on him. "A few days ago you called me. 'Hello, Con,' you said. 'How'd you like to go out with me?'

"'Sure,' I responded.

"'Great,' you said. 'I'll think up someplace fun to go, then call you with the details.'

"I was thrilled, but you never called back until, let's see, two hours ago. Then you said you'd pick me up around 7:00 and didn't show up until almost 8:00. And so, I just sat there, wondering if you would even come at all . . . feeling very foolish. Then my mind began to play games with me: 'What if he got in an accident? Is he okay? Maybe he isn't interested in me anymore. Maybe he's out with someone else. Does he think the world revolves around him—and that I'm supposed to just wait here by the phone? What an insensitive jerk!'"

Connie moved forward and locked eyes with Bob. "If you really care about me, then show some respect. Above all . . . talk to me!"

Bob just sat at the table with his mouth wide open—at a complete loss for words.

Sigmund Freud admitted, "The great question I have not been able to answer is, what does a woman want?"

To many guys it's still a mystery today. So, exactly what do women want from men? Actually, many of the same things men want. Here are some clues.

THEY WANT YOU TO SHARE YOUR FEELINGS

Women care about what you're thinking and want you to include them in your personal life. So go ahead, talk.

- How was that game/fishing trip with the guys? What did you do? What kinds of topics did you talk about?
- How did you feel when the boss handed over his biggest account to you?
- What did you think about that movie?
- How was church?
- How do you feel about our relationship at this point?

THEY WANT YOUR ATTENTION

"Michael?! Michael . . . are you listening to me?"

I've been asked this question countless times in my life by parents, teachers, teens I work with today—even by the women I've dated. In addition to opening up and spilling your guts, the people around you—especially the women you date—need you to take an interest in their world. Above all, you need to close your mouth from time to time and listen.

In his book *Born for Love,* Dr. Leo Buscaglia has this to say about the art of listening . . . and giving others your attention:

> A student once told me that there were times when she felt that the entire world was deaf to the sound of her voice. "I get no response. I speak and end up feeling that I am talking to myself. Am I going mad?"

Most of us have experienced the emptiness that comes from feeling tuned out. Listening is an act of love, or at a more basic level, an act of simple consideration.

All communication requires two basic things, a speaking voice and a listening ear. This sounds pretty simple, but it's not. Most of us are very selective listeners, tuning in and tuning out as our interest dictates. With all the extraneous noise and worthless static that bombards us daily, this type of non-listening can be a blessing. It is something else, however, when we find ourselves tuning out those we say we love.

THEY WANT YOU TO WATCH THOSE WOUNDING WORDS

Mark Twain once said he could go for two months on a good compliment. Likewise, every one of us needs to be appreciated, to be applauded for the awesome and unique person God made in us. We need others to recognize our strengths or sometimes just to prop us up in the places where we tend to lean a little. Honest compliments are simple and cost nothing to give, but we must not underestimate their worth.

On the flip side of the coin, there is nothing more destructive to a relationship than a thoughtless put-down.

- "I wouldn't even think about ordering dessert if I were you. (Hey, just kidding . . . lighten up!)"
- "Yeah, that's a nice new dress . . . although you look a bit like the 'Highlighter Girl.'"
- "Oh, it's that time of the month again. I'll avoid you until you become human again, okay?!"
- "Hey, you go off to that 'Celebrating Womanhood' class and do your girl thing—or whatever it is you ladies do. The guys and I have an important game anyway."
- "That's just like a woman—you're all mechanically reclined. Look, leave the technical stuff to a man, okay?"

WHAT MEN SHOULD KNOW

How can men bridge communication gaps and deepen understanding of women? Susie and I took this question to females all across North America. Here's what they said.

"Give me a sympathetic ear." A woman views conversation as a way of sharing her emotions with a listener, unlike men who see it as a way of defining a problem and finding a solution. Barbara of Boise, Idaho, says, "More often than not, I want your attention—not your advice."

"I want to be heard." Next to being a good listener, a woman needs the man in her life to understand what she's communicating. "Don't just nod your head a few times and think you're doing me a favor," says Tess of Virginia Beach, Virginia. "I need you to hear my heart and connect with me. Above all, show me that you really care about what I'm thinking and feeling."

"Let me know I'm needed." While a man derives self-esteem by being respected, a woman feels worthy when she is loved and cherished. Kathy of Salina, Kansas, sums it up this way: "It hurts when I'm neglected or not taken seriously by my boyfriend. I want him to show me that I'm not second-rate in his life. I need to know I'm special to him."

"Give me some strokes—please!" A woman gains a deeper sense of self-worth and identity from the reassurance of those around her—especially a man. And, yes, this includes compliments. "Even the most successful or beautiful woman can feel as though she comes up short at times," says Connie of Pasadena, California. "Give me some positive feedback on a regular basis: 'You look great in that dress' or 'You made a good decision at work.'"

"Never underestimate my abilities." Women are serious about their accomplishments and goals—and that includes everything from their jobs to their home lives. Just as a man

gains his identity and status from his achievements, the same often holds true for a woman. "A man's condescending or patronizing attitude toward my abilities is a big turnoff," says Vanessa of New York City.

"Sometimes, I want to be alone." Women—like men—need "down time" to shop, read, recharge batteries. A man shouldn't feel upset if the woman in his life doesn't want to spend every free minute with him. "Don't be possessive and don't cling to me," says Anita of Baton Rouge, Louisiana. "Give me some space from time to time."

Communication is the key to any relationship. If both parties don't communicate immediately or at least when it's feasibly possible when one feels hurt or when one sees a problem, problems grow and the couple grow apart. If the lack of communication continues too long, the couple will eventually stop communicating altogether and the relationship disintegrates—sometimes without either one knowing why. Address problems right away so that doesn't happen to you.

CHAPTER 12

Keys to Understanding

Hoards of frantic tourists darting in every direction ... cramped waiting areas ... high-priced, "gas-'n'-sip"-style airport food. It was all behind me now. I had caught my connecting flight (and survived the jet-set jungle).

As the DC–10 lifted into the "friendly skies" over Dallas, I tilted my seat back and soaked in the convenience of modern-day travel: frantic flight attendants racing in every direction ... cramped quarters ... high-cholesterol, cardboard-tasting airplane food! (Okay, I confess—I'd rather have my teeth drilled than endure a plane trip.)

But after a quick hop through the stratosphere, I'd be on the ground in Kansas City. I was on assignment with *Breakaway* and enroute to Six Flags Worlds of Fun theme park. I had planned to catch some roller coasters, snap a few pictures, and compare the ups and downs of our wild rides with the Christian walk. (It was ideal material for a teen magazine—not to mention a good excuse to ride a few roller coasters!)

While the kid in me couldn't wait for the fun, the serious grown-up side of me occasionally snapped back to reality. I was hopelessly preoccupied with scary, roller-coaster emotions rumbling through my heart. (I'm talking about romantic feelings, not heartburn ... but I realize the two are sometimes indistinguishable!)

I glanced out the window and studied the Texas landscape below—flat, monotonous . . . void (a perfect picture of my love life). *Lord, why isn't it like it used to be—back when I was wide-eyed in junior high? Why are relationships so hard at this stage of my life? The minute I think I've found the right woman, the second I'm positive it's true love . . . WHOOOSH! . . . either my heart takes a nosedive and I pull away, or she rejects me. I don't get it.*

I took a sip of my Pawberry Punch and crunched on a piece of ice. *Lord, I'm gonna bug you once more about Alison. Is this the right woman for me? She's convinced we're perfect for each other—and won't even let breakup change her heart (we've been through two together). But me? I just don't know.*

I glanced out the window again. The sky was gray in all directions. Visibility was zero. *Maybe I'm the one who's wrong. Maybe she's right . . . just right for me. Maybe I'm about to miss what could be the greatest blessing of my life.*

Suddenly, the plane encountered heavy turbulence and the "Fasten Seatbelt" sign began to flash.

"The captain just turned on the seatbelt sign," a voice over the intercom redundantly announced. "Looks like we hit some rough air."

Ah ha, I thought. *It's a sign. Lord, you don't want me to date this girl.*

Then I realized how ridiculous that kind of reasoning was . . . and I remembered other so-called signs I had encountered. A few months after Alison and I broke up, I spent many devotional times praying for a relationship with the *right* one. Occasionally, I received a note in the mail from Alison, suggesting we talk (usually about getting back together).

It's a sign, I'd tell myself. *Maybe the Lord wants us together after all.*

I chomped on another piece of ice and sat back in my seat. *Forgive me, Lord. You just don't work that way ... especially when it comes to important matters like marriage. Please help me to know your direction—clearly.*

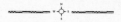

I'm convinced that the two most important decisions we'll ever make in life involve the heart: (1) committing it to Jesus, and (2) committing it to a life mate in marriage.

I've taken care of the first decision. It's the second one that's giving me troubles. Frankly, it's not as cut-and-dried. After all, marriage isn't the ticket to eternity, and we won't find wholeness through a wedding ring. What's more, God can—and will (if we let him)—use us as singles just as much, if not more, than if we decide to marry.

But nonetheless, the desire to share life intimately with another person usually pounds in the heart of every healthy single. (This could be one reason why you're reading this book.)

Finding the *right* person is another matter—often a very difficult matter.

As you head out on this great adventure, swinging through the jungle of singleness—occasionally latching onto the vine of another native (a potential life mate)—what moves can you make to ensure your success—and survival? In other words, what can you do to keep from making the wrong decision and spending the rest of your life with the wrong person?

Let's flash back about fifteen years and pretend we're all sitting in front of my fireplace, and I'm telling you a bedtime story.

The answers are found in the keys....

KEYS TO THE HEART

"Rough water ahead—HOLD ON!" shouts the jungle guide.

Prince Philip grips the side of the canoe as it tears through a mound of twisted branches clogging the narrow river. Brightly colored birds dart in every direction. Boa constrictors hang from branches. Lizards and alligators scamper into dense brush lining the shore.

Thunk . . . thunk.

The boat begins to rock violently, but the young prince doesn't bat an eye. The temple is in sight—peeking through a tangled canopy of leaves and vines. His long journey will soon be over. Once ashore, Philip pulls out his machete and slices through the thick brush. Minutes later, he uncovers a rocky path leading to the ancient place.

The prince is ready to marry and has many women to choose from. But before he selects a bride, Philip knows he must possess the jungle's most valuable treasure: the sacred "Keys to the Heart." There is only one place to find them— Ashbul, the wise and holy priest.

"Come in. I've been expecting you," Ashbul greets Philip.

"Then you know what I've come for."

"What every young prince and princess desires."

Ashbul holds up four keys, each inscribed with different names: "Prayer," "Honesty," "Information," "Communication."

Then he leans close to Philip. "These can unlock the secrets to lifelong happiness . . . but only if you choose to let them. Listen carefully."

The priest carefully explains the meaning of each key: "First, get on your knees before the Lord and pray. Pray hard. Then, search your heart. Discover what is real in there and what is false. Get rid of the lies—and pray hard. Then, learn. Learn everything you can about the other and everything about yourself. Then pray even harder. Finally, and above all, talk . . . and pray hard. Then, talk some more . . . and pray hard again.

"Now go and take these keys with you. And find your princess, Philip."

Key #1: Prayer

When it comes to matters of the heart, too many people forget to turn on their brains—the body part that actually handles the cognitive/thinking processes. Look at the reasons why some individuals have chosen to take the plunge instead of using their brains:

- "Cupid shot his arrow and passion took over." (Ahhh, a case of "Urgetomergehormonalscreaminitis.")
- "This is probably my only chance to ever wear a wedding ring." (Classic "Insecuresoigottasettlemania.")
- "I'm tired of waiting. Besides, anything has got to be better than going solo." (Contagious "Impatientclocktickin" syndrome.)

God has some better reasons:

So God created man in his own image, in the image of God he created him; male and female he created them. God blessed them and said to them, 'Be fruitful and increase in number' (Genesis 1:27–28).

Trust the LORD with all your heart, and don't depend on your own understanding. Remember the LORD in all you do, and he will give you success. Don't depend on your own wisdom. Respect the LORD and refuse to do wrong (Proverbs 3:5–7 NCV).

Enjoy serving the LORD, and he will give you what you want (Psalm 37:4 NCV).

Kirk—a single friend of mine—had this to say about dating and relationships—not to mention the mistakes he has made: "Every blunder you can possibly make in the romance department, I'm guilty of making. I've been engaged twice, for the wrong reasons (both times).

"I've finally come to this conclusion: Marriage is a great blessing, and I desire to be a husband. But until I fulfill that dream, I'm committing every relationship I encounter to prayer. That's the first and last place to be."

What to pray for:

- clear direction regarding a certain individual
- understanding of the opposite sex
- guidance as you seek to sort through doubts, fears, and red flags concerning a relationship
- that he prepares you for the right *type* of person to marry

What not to pray for:

- that God makes you or your partner fall head over heels in love
- that he smooths out every rough edge in a potential partner
- that the Lord change another person to make him/her fit your idea of an ideal mate
- that God send you the special person he has in mind for you (it's better to seek a type of person)

Key #2: Honesty

"Who am I?"

When you were a teenager, you probably spent some time gazing into a mirror, trying to figure out this mystery. For me, it went something like this:

I am the youngest of six—the baby in the family (that's how my jealous brothers and sisters often referred to me). I am the son of Ronald Ross and Ruth Johnson. We are part

Swedish, part Dutch. I am creative. I am a writer and an artist. I am an animal lover and a nature nut ...

As I grew older, I found myself adding much more to the list. My interests, abilities, opinions, and values were slowly redefined—eventually shaping who I am today. (And the list continues to change.) But as I grew, especially when I began dating, I discovered that occasionally I'd hide behind masks. Psychologists say it's normal to a certain degree and refer to it as a "survival" mechanism. But when it comes to intimate relationships, it's quite a different matter. You can't change the rules once you're married. So the answer hinges on starting out honestly—without masks.

So, let me re-ask the question: Who are *you*?

Are you trying to be someone you're not because you think it will increase your chances of finding and keeping love?

Too many people, including me, think that if they pretend to be someone they're not, they will get what they ultimately desire: a life mate. But pay close attention: This is a course headed for disaster. If you're pretending to be someone else, you're going to attract and possibly get the wrong person.

A better approach: *Be the best person you can be.* This way, you stand a greater chance of attracting someone else who is seeking to be the best person he/she can be.

Key #3: Information

If you were to make as nearly an objective and complete evaluation of yourself as possible, what would you say? Most psychologists describe the human personality in terms of observable behaviors. But you're also made up of inner, subjective qualities.

Galen, one of the great medical doctors the world has known—born in Greece a century after the death of Christ—based his theories about personality traits on the fluids in the body. He concluded that everyone can be classified into four main types.

Sanguine: From the word *sanguis,* meaning "blood." Someone who hopes for the best or is confidently optimistic is a sanguine person. Other traits: cheerful, hearty, outgoing, sturdy, fearless, and primarily interested in physical pleasures.

Phlegmatic: From the Greek word *phlegma,* which means "flame" or "inflammation." Phlegm is the white mucus that you cough up when you have a cold. A person described this way is said to be slow, cold, aloof, calm, detached, quiet, withdrawn, dependable, and unemotional.

Choler: From the Greek word meaning "bile." A choleric person is someone readily given to anger and fits of temper.

Melancholic: From the Greek word, which means "black." This type of person is predominantly cynical, "a realist," and frequently is sad and unhappy.

According to Galen, all human beings fall into one of these four categories with some overlapping. With this in mind, what's your personality style or dominant trait? Having a firm grasp on this information will affect who you attract and to whom you're attracted.

Key #4: Communication

When I returned from my trip to Kansas City, I sat down with Alison and had a long, sober, heart-to-heart talk about our relationship . . . and why I had doubts about its working. I didn't hold back and neither did she.

Then we both participated in an exercise together. We pulled out pieces of notepaper and made two lists: one titled "I Am Mostly . . ." and the other titled "You Are Mostly . . ." The goal was threefold: (1) to help us get a better picture of who we are—including our strengths and weaknesses, (2) to help us determine how compatible we were, and (3) to get each other thinking and talking about the type of person we believe to be an ideal match for a life mate.

We didn't walk away from the exercise with a specific course of action in mind such as breakup or makeup. But it did get us talking . . . and gave us some information to work with.

The next step was to go back where we started: on our knees in prayer.

My list looked something like this:
"I Am Mostly . . ."

- a person who loves children
- family-oriented
- dependable/loyal
- zany/fun-loving
- adventurous
- easy to talk to
- easygoing

"You Are Mostly . . ."

- a person who loves children
- family-oriented
- dependable/loyal
- a realist/impersonal
- a homebody
- solitary/quiet
- inflexible

TIPS FROM THE JUNGLE

Once you're past the initial me-can't-swing-without-this-Tarzan/Jane creature emotional high of a new romance, ask yourself some serious questions:

- How much does he/she listen to me?
- Does this person share my values?

- Do we talk about things that matter or is it always fluff?
- What are his/her life goals?
- What is his/her idea of a solid home? How about parenting beliefs?

Pick this person's brain about everything. Ask questions and learn as much as you can about your date. The right information is the key to understanding.

Be honest with yourself and each other! Remember: Unspoken, unshared visions set you up for disaster.

Don't hold back ... earnestly seek to communicate. This takes patience, sensitivity, and a good ear.

PART FOUR:

Basic Training

CHAPTER 13

Becoming the Mate Your Future Spouse Will Need

Check the most important qualities you're looking for in a mate:

___man/woman of integrity
___physical beauty
___great body
___good sense of humor
___money
___involved in local church
___godly
___tender heart

Most of us have a good idea of the kind of person with whom we want to spend the rest of our lives. And when you meet that person, you'll want him/her to immediately possess several of the qualities you've dreamed about.

But what about you? Are you becoming the kind of spouse your mate will need? If we want a husband or wife of integrity, it's important that we become men and women of integrity now. If we want someone who's involved in church, then *we* need to become active in our local church. In other words, is it fair to carry specific expectations of our future mate if we're not willing to become what we're looking for?

Besides being a man who loves God with all his heart, my future husband needs to be patient and understanding with me. So, it only makes sense that *I* start working on those qualities right now in my own life.

I'm an extremely impatient woman, and up to this point, I have never asked for patience for fear the Lord would give it to me. But doesn't it make sense that if I want a husband who's patient, I need to develop the same quality in my own life? So I'm trying desperately to be more patient with those around me, more understanding when friends don't meet my expectations, and more forgiving when others disappoint me.

It's hard. But I want to be the godly woman my future husband will need. That also means I can't wait until we meet to deepen my relationship with God. My walk with God has to be an alive, growing, vital part of my life right now. And that happens not simply because of my future husband—it happens because God is number one in my life. Realistically, I know there's a possibility I may never marry. If that happens, I still want a deep relationship with my Father. So now is the time for spiritual growth.

Singles have a tendency to wait to get ready for a possible marriage. "When I meet someone I really like, then I'll start working out."

"If I was dating someone, I'd be happy. But right now I'm not happy and don't feel like trying."

"I know I need to get more involved in church. One of these days, I will."

Let's quit putting off what we could be doing. Think about what kind of spouse you want to be for your future mate, and start becoming one now.

MIXED MESSAGES

"The American male is the most insecure species on earth!"

That statement was made by a single female friend of mine who works in the travel industry. She has crisscrossed the globe many times and, consequently, has dated all kinds of men.

"When I finally settle down, I think it'll be with a European," she told me. "Probably a Frenchman. Not only are they great romantics, but they understand the ingredients of what makes a real man."

Okay, so her comments are a little extreme, but I think she makes a pretty good point. The fact is, we live in the most stressed-out culture on the face of the earth. Everyone's in a big hurry to attain the "American Dream." We have important places to be and impressive goals to achieve: promotions, titles, awards, material possessions. And once we've arrived, are we happy? No. The grass is greener on the other side . . . right?

Add to this frenzied race the expectations we must live up to. Every day, we're bombarded with an unhealthy menu of mixed messages from TV shows, movies, books, music, even computer programs. Our brains are constantly pumped with the same lies:

- "You're nothing unless you possess a bank vault bursting with bucks, have the IQ of Einstein, and are blessed with a terrific body."
- "Look out for numero uno."
- "Go for the gusto and get all you can . . .'cause you only live once."
- "Stop dancin' with the dinosaurs . . . purity was lost somewhere back in the Jurassic period!"

The result? Insecurity.

As the youngest boy of four boys and two girls, I grew up thinking it was unmasculine to be tender, or show weakness, or cry. So did Keith, a single man from Nashville.

"The lies I was fed growing up really messed up my identity as a man," he says. "I began to think I was weird because I was creative and not athletic. I didn't come to grips with this until I was in my twenties."

BEWARE OF THE *GLAMOUR* GIRL!

The so-called "Women's Liberation Movement" doesn't make matters any easier. Sex roles are often blurred. What was once valued in the past is sometimes frowned upon today.

For example, an article in *Glamour* magazine cautioned women to "Beware of the man who does a lot of ritual performance: You Girl, Me Boy; here's candy, here's flowers; here's where we're going for dinner."

The author went on to say, "Look closely and you'll see he's too busy choreographing the mating dance to really get to know you. It's tempting to let the man take charge of the wooing, but later on he'll expect to take charge of your marriage in the same way he took charge of the courtship."

Compare that to what contemporary Christian artist Cindy Morgan says she looks for in a potential mate:

"I expect him to take charge. After all, it's biblical for a man to be a leader. Men who can't make up their minds about anything or take charge of a situation drive me crazy! Wanna know what makes a real man? Study the life of Jesus. He is the ultimate example."

Cindy's right. For all of us—men *and* women—Jesus is the Light, the Hope, and our ultimate Model of true godliness. When he walked the earth 2000 years ago and touched the lives of his followers, they were changed forever. Not one of them would ever forget their three-year experience with the Master.

Dr. William Fletcher, a minister in Colorado and author of *The Second Greatest Command,* points out some of the key ways Jesus stood as a solid example of a single adult living a holy life:

- Jesus was genuinely concerned about others—their families, homes, and health.
- Jesus was willing to take time for people in need even though he was engaged in a busy ministry.
- Jesus provided faithful support in the spiritual battle by intercessory prayer.
- Jesus extended complete forgiveness, even when it seemed undeserved.
- Jesus humbly served his followers, exemplified in his washing their feet.
- Jesus ultimately gave himself for us in his death on Calvary's cross.

QUALITIES OF A GODLY MAN/WOMAN

A lot goes into the making of a godly single adult—more than can fit in one chapter. But here are six keys to authentic holiness. And if you want to prepare now to be the kind of spouse your future mate needs, working on these ingredients is the place to start.

Godly Men and Women Follow God's Example

The one man I've sought to model my life after is a pastor named Andy Abbas. Why? Because Andy modeled his life after Christ.

Shortly after I graduated from college and was plunged into my first real job as a journalist, Andy took me under his wing and discipled me. That lasted for three years—a period of deep spiritual growth.

Andy was everything *I* wanted to be as a man: a faithful husband and committed father, a man of solid integrity, a man of compassion, a servant of God who would lay down his life for others.

When you met Andy, you also had an encounter with Jesus. And that's what I want others to say about me. The key: Follow the footsteps of the King and seek his will for your life.

> Be imitators of God, therefore, as dearly loved children and live a life of love, just as Christ loved us and gave himself up for us as a fragrant offering and sacrifice to God. (Ephesians 5:1–2)

Godly Men and Women Serve Others

"If anyone asks the question, 'How can I be a happy Christian?' our Lord's answer is very simple," writes Andrew Murray in his book *The True Vine*. "'You cannot have My joy without My life. Abide in Me, and let Me abide in you, and My joy will be in you.'"

Andrew goes on to explain that abiding in Jesus—and experiencing true joy—comes when we follow our Lord's example and step out as servants.

"Take up your work, then, you who seem to be the nobodies, the drudges, the maid-of-all-work, the clerk, or shop assistant," author F. B. Meyer explains in his book *Devotional Commentary*. "Do it with a brave heart, looking up to Him who for many years toiled at the carpenter's bench. Amid the many scenes and actions of life, set the Lord always before your face. Do all as in His presence, and to win His smile; and be sure to cultivate a spirit of love to God and man. Look out for opportunities of cheering your fellow-workers . . . so the lowliest service will glisten."

The key: Take your eyes off yourself and see how you can meet the needs of others.

> Do nothing out of selfish ambition or vain conceit, but in humility consider others better than yourselves. Each of you should look not only to your own interests, but also to the interests of others (Philippians 2:3–4).

Godly Men and Women Have Convictions

Knowing right from wrong doesn't make someone a person of conviction. Those values have to be exercised and tested before they really work. Anything worth valuing—especially if it's one of God's values—will get Satan's attention. The deceiver wants to convince us that acting on God's standards is too tough, too demanding, and too stupid if you want to have a social life.

The key: Stand firm in what you believe and don't give up, buying the lie that you just can't measure up. Your future spouse needs a mate of integrity.

> Whatever happens, conduct yourselves in a manner worthy of the gospel of Christ. Then, whether I come and see you or only hear about you in my absence, I will know that you stand firm in one spirit, contending as one man for the faith of the gospel without being frightened in any way by those who oppose you (Philippians 1:27–28).

Godly Men and Women Are Secure

That's because they aren't afraid to admit their weaknesses. Let's face it—all of us have twinges of insecurity about ourselves. But godly adults—those who allow the Holy Spirit to transform their weaknesses into strengths—derive their security from their relationship with God. If we're serious about being holy men and women and preparing now to be the spouse our future mate will need . . . then we'll strive to become secure individuals. Like my friend Cheryl. There are several things in her life that shout security to me and make me want to imitate these specific areas. These are the specifics I see in her life that are true models of security: She doesn't tear down others to build up herself; she forgives those who may never have the courage to apologize; instead of being insulted by the garbage someone else was dealt in life, she strives to recycle it into a blessing by helping them see how God can make something good happen from something bad; instead of being threatened by talented people, she's inspired by them; she lives a life of integrity—her private life and her public life are one and the same; she realizes that people are more important than projects and plans.

The key: Don't hide behind a polished facade or draw your sense of self-worth from possessions, position, or power. Build your foundation on the solid rock—faith in Jesus Christ.

> His divine power has given us everything we need for
> life and godliness through our knowledge of him who
> called us by his own glory and goodness (2 Peter 1:3).

Godly Men and Women Take Responsibility

Instead of blaming their failures on someone else, godly singles admit that their actions don't always match their convictions. Too often, we think that by saying the words, "I blew it," we're somehow weaker. Actually, just the opposite is true. Everyone admires someone who has the courage to admit his/her mistakes.

James 4:7 reads, "Submit yourselves, then, to God. Resist the devil, and he will flee from you." According to popular author Ken Abraham, "Most of us, in our misguided ideas of macho self-sufficiency, have reversed the order at times, only to suffer humiliating defeat. Then, after being thoroughly embarrassed, we blame the boss, the territory, or even God for our failures, frustrations and foolishness."

The key: Take over your actions and make every effort to become self-controlled.

> For you died, and your life is now hidden with Christ in God. When Christ, who is your life, appears, then you also will appear with him in glory (Colossians 3:3–4).

Godly Men and Women Have Control

No, not the control over others, people, money, and cars you hear about from the media. Godly singles want self-control over themselves. They know it's the eternally self-indulgent who say yes to their urges.

The key: Holy men and women know the *what, when,* and *how* to say no.

> Each of you should learn to control his own body in a way that is holy and honorable, not in passionate lust like the heathen, who do not know God (1 Thessalonians 4:4–5).

Godly Men and Women Make Every Effort Not to Lose Their Temper

Notice how the tiniest things can sometimes trigger fiery eruptions of emotion usually at the worst possible moments?

- A colleague at work—one you perceive as being more talented than you—makes a suggestion about improving a project you completed. Suddenly, a deep-seated insecurity raises its ugly head . . . and you let him have it.

- Your date tells you that he/she isn't so crazy about a particular restaurant you've picked out. "Just call me Mr. Bad Taste!" you roar. "I can't seem to do anything right. Next time, Ms. Perfect, you decide where we're going to eat."
- A car cuts you off on the highway. "Idiot!" you scream out the window. "Where'd you get your license . . . from a Cracker Jack box?" It's a good thing you don't have one of those Christian fish symbols on your bumper.

According to author Gary Smalley, hot tempers of this kind often result from anger stored deep in our hearts. "Anger can emerge in the form of hurt feelings, fear, or frustrating stress," he says. "Every unforgiven ember of hurt or frustration can build into a lava flow of anger, which can block you from knowing God better. If you would humble yourself, admit your offensive ways, and seek forgiveness from others, it could be the start of a major renewal in your life." And you'll do your future spouse a big favor.

What can you do to stop the flow of anger? Here are some tips:

1. When you're angry, admit it to God. Ask him to help you get your head on straight so you can sort through the problem.
2. Decrease your expectations from the things God created and increase your focus on God himself—the giver of eternal life, joy, love, and rest.
3. Try to help others gain release from their anger. Approach the people you've offended and try to drain from them as much resentment as possible.

The key: Don't let hurt and anger fester inside . . . deal with it calmly and rationally. Above all, be patient and tenderhearted.

A wise man fears the LORD and shuns evil, but a fool is hotheaded and reckless. A quick-tempered man does foolish things, and a crafty man is hated (Proverbs 14:16–17).

Godly Men and Women Understand God's Grace

"The paint is still wet, and you're still under construction. But take a good, hard look in the mirror. God's creating a masterpiece in you!"

That's an important bit of encouragement I try to instill in the teens I disciple at my church . . . especially when they blow it in their walk with Christ. Though most teens know that God is always forgiving, their hearts don't grasp how much God is on their team. Godly singles understand their heavenly Father is unfailingly persistent.

God isn't shaking his finger at us when we blow it. Instead, he picks us up, dusts us off, encourages us to keep trying, and points us onward and upward. That's how grace works for the believer—it motivates us to keep moving. Not understanding his grace grinds us to a halt.

God's Solid Promises

The LORD is faithful to all his promises and loving toward all he has made (Psalm 145:13b).

Be on your guard; stand firm in the faith; be men of courage; be strong (1 Corinthians 16:13).

I am the vine; you are the branches. If a man remains in me and I in him, he will bear much fruit; apart from me you can do nothing (John 15:5).

The key: Live by God's Word and his grace.

From the fullness of his grace we have all received one blessing after another. For the law was given through Moses; grace and truth came through Jesus Christ (John 1:16–17).

Becoming the future mate your spouse will need means developing godly virtues such as patience, responsibility, compassion, self-discipline, courage, perseverance, honesty, loyalty, and faith. Only by developing these traits first can we become whole persons, ready to enter into a healthy marriage.

CHAPTER 14

From the Heart of a Woman

There are specific times in a woman's life when her needs and expectations change. But woven throughout those changes are constants that men can count on. Let's look at what comes, what goes, and what remains the same.

SHIFTING MOODS

Not every woman experiences PMS (*pre-* or *post-menstrual syndrome*), but many do. And for those around them, life can be downright frightening.

I'd never been around anyone who actually had PMS until I graduated from college and moved away from home. I was a youth minister in a medium-sized church and quickly became friends with a family who lived closeby.

Rebecca was funny, creative, and an extremely giving wife and mother. Everyone loved being with her . . . except around the tenth of every month. She transformed into a completely different person! Her humor vanished and biting sarcasm surfaced. Her patience sailed out the door and anger took over. Her talkative personality switched to a quiet, depressed spirit.

For a long time she struggled with PMS symptoms without knowing what it was. Instead, she questioned her faith, her walk with God, and her emotional stability.

About ten years later, when she finally realized what was happening, she was able to get help controlling her mood swings.

Steer Clear

For Rebecca, caffeine was a major ingredient that aggravated her mood swings. So about a week before, during, and after, she cut back on her coffee intake. It made a difference.

She also realized that she needed to stay away from stressful situations as much as possible during her period. It was not a good time for decision making because of her mood swings, so she made an effort to steer clear of activities that required her to make decisions—or she put off making them for about a week until she could think more clearly without being affected by depression.

She began taking B-complex vitamins to restore the necessary nutrients a woman's body is naturally deprived of during the menstrual cycle. And again, it made a difference.

How This Applies to Women

Women, take inventory of your own personality. If you become sarcastic during your period, make an effort to think before you speak. You'll save some friendships this way. If you become hyper, involve yourself in athletic activity, such as walking, aerobics, or video exercises, so your extra energy will be directed in positive action instead of negative action aimed at friends and relatives.

All this requires getting to know yourself. Learn to recognize your own body signals and understand what incidents or people put you in stressful situations. Many times it's difficult to realize what you need or how people are perceiving you once you're in the situation. Consider asking a close friend to help you monitor your actions during this time of the month, so she can help you see your actions, mood swings, or hyper-activity, and work with you to create optional solutions.

What Does It Really Mean?

I've only recently begun to experience PMS symptoms. I guess it's different for every woman. For me, PMS means literally, "please, more sweets." About once a month I need them. For you, it might mean "please, more solitude."

PMS victims are often hardest on those closest to them. That's why, during specific times of the month, friendships and relationships can really be strained—especially new dating relationships. But I've recently discovered the perfect date—the perfect man. He's a Keebler elf. He knows what I really want! COOKIES. Just give me cookies and cake every three or four weeks, and I'm happy.

LIFE CHANGES

There are also other seasons in a woman's life in which her needs shift and even change completely. Often people will say that single women who are successful in their careers are too career-oriented. I want to yell, "Well, I'm single! What else am I going to throw myself into?"

We could all get part-time jobs at Taco Tim's, but then we'd probably hear, "She just doesn't have any goals in life." How can we win?

Though there are times when we are extremely career-oriented, there are other times we'd love not having to worry about making money, paying bills, or moving up the corporate ladder. These desires can easily change with our fluctuating moods.

Though the situations of our lives vary, there are a few things that never change—and these are the things we always need—no matter what season of life we're in.

Respect

Men, please listen closely. Even if we are independent and successful, every woman wants a man to respect her. We want to know that you value us as women and as individuals. Common courtesies such as opening doors, helping us out of the car, taking our coats, and pulling out our chairs go a long way in communicating value and respect. What woman doesn't feel special when a guy does those things for her? But respect goes both ways. Women should treat men courteously also.

Punctuality

Women need and want males to be men of their word. We're frustrated if you tell us to be ready by a specific time, yet you don't arrive for another twenty minutes without calling to explain you're going to be late.

It matters when men, or women for that matter, don't keep their word. We need and want men to be on time.

Knowing His Role

Another unchanging need of women is for men to know and live out their proper God-designed roles. Our Creator has designed the male to be the leader in relationships. And because we were designed by the same God, women need men to take the initiative.

One of the most frustrating things for me as a woman is going out with a guy who says, "Well, what do you want to do?" When I hear that, I start thinking, *I'd like to go back home, please.*

If a guy doesn't care enough about the woman he's asked out to think ahead and actually plan an evening, then he's not taking the initiative God intended for him. I'm not saying we want men to say, "This is what we're doing whether you like it or not!" We want to give input and share ideas from time to time, but we also need to know that you're clear and confident in your role as leader. It makes us feel secure and comfortable about being with you.

Pursued or Pursuer?

Again, because God created man to be the aggressor, we women want to be pursued. A lot of us have our roles mixed up. I have several female friends who really go after guys . . . calling them, chasing them, asking them out. Though it sounds old-fashioned, I believe God designed man to go after woman. And when a woman takes over that role, she's robbed that particular guy of his initiative.

Karen met Jason at a large business party. Both were attractive and single, and it didn't take them long to gravitate to each other during the evening. Karen was immediately "in like" with Jason, and as they laughed and chatted the evening away, she found herself hoping he'd ask for her phone number.

Toward the end of the evening, he reached into his lapel pocket, handed her his business card and told her to give him a call. She smiled, accepted the card, and went home dreaming of Jason.

After a few days, she phoned his office and was told he was on another line. She left her number but he didn't return the call.

She phoned again the next day, and after being put on hold, was informed he was very busy. She phoned again and was told he couldn't speak with her.

Three weeks passed, and they ran into each other at another business event. He took her home after the party but never went out with her again.

What happened? Way back when Jason gave Karen his business card, he was relinquishing his right to be the aggressor and placing that role on her. If Karen had recognized this, she could have quickly and easily set the roles straight. She could have refused the card and said, "I'm not comfortable calling men, but I don't mind if you call me." The responsibility of pursuing would have been rightly placed on Jason. If interested, he would have pursued.

---·◇·---

Many things change in a woman's life: her body, her career, her feelings, and her moods . . . but the need for a man to be the initiator, arrive when he says he will, respect her, and to be comfortable in his God-designed role are needs that will never change. They are the constant, predictable traits that women want from men.

CHAPTER 15

From the Heart of a Man

Brent Cleary, my accountability partner, sat across the table sipping a cup of coffee and thumbing his Bible, looking for a photocopied article he had stuffed in the back.

I glanced out my kitchen window. The sun wasn't even up yet. It was just after 6:00. For a couple hours every Friday morning, Brent and I yank off our masks and get down to some deep discussions and tear-filled prayer. And trust me, our discussions get intense.

"Found it!" Brent said. "Mike, it's pretty serious stuff but something every man needs to hear. It's by Dr. Archibald Hart and is titled 'Sex Under Control.' Listen as I read it. . . ."

I was moved by what Brent read and believe every man and woman should hear it, too. So I reprinted it below.

Okay, guys and ladies, shut the door, pour a cup of coffee and start reading. . . .

SEX UNDER CONTROL

Two days before writing this, I opened a letter from a single woman only 21 years old. She wrote she has never had sex and has never been abused. But she is deathly afraid of men and their sexuality. She had read my recently published book,

The Sexual Man, and wanted to let me know that my description of how men behave these days was right on target. "Men," she writes, "are obsessed with sex. Girls don't feel safe around men anymore." Her comments about male sexuality did not surprise me. What did alarm me was her suggestion that God had made a mistake when He designed males the way that they are. God doesn't make mistakes, but the effect of sin has left many men in a sexuality crisis.

Sexuality Today

What is the state of male sexuality today? To answer this question, I obtained detailed responses to an extensive questionnaire from 600 men. I sought out "good" men—men who are mainstream, married, monogamous, and mainly religious. Many are pastors. I wanted to know the deep, honest, no-holds-barred feelings of "good" men about their sexuality.

Many of the 600 God-fearing, family-loving men I studied wrote me a letter or scribbled comments on the sides of their questionnaire. Many had the same theme: "Am I like other men?" "Am I different?" "Am I normal sexually?"

There were also variations on this theme. Questions like, "Why does God let me suffer from such strong sexual urges?" "Why do I feel so guilty about sex?"

Some reported that their wives had said things like: "You know, you really are over-sexed. I think there's something wrong with you. Why don't you go see a doctor or get some help for yourself?" Many had been made to feel like they were sex-crazed sexual perverts. One pastor wrote, "God must have a warped sense of humor to put so much sexual desire in me and so little in my wife!"

Are these men who struggle with a very strong sex drive abnormal? No. Some may have a little more testosterone circulating in their veins than others, but the bottom line is if you are a healthy, average male, you will have a pretty powerful desire for sex. Just accept it.

It's not a man's desire for sex that is the problem. It is how this need has become contaminated or distorted. Abnor-

mality has to do with how men seek to express this drive—
what satisfies it and what doesn't. It is here that something ter-
ribly distorting has happened to male sexuality.

Most Christian men face a lifelong struggle controlling
their sexuality. The struggle is basically between their hormones and higher aspirations, between their bodies and their
fallenness. Good, God-fearing men have a greater struggle
than worldly men for obvious reasons. Godless men don't think
there is any problem. "Sex is all good," they say. "We've just
messed it up by attributing too many morals to it." If many of
them had it their way, sex would be a free-for-all, no-conse-
quences-or-responsibilities playground. And women would be
the losers.

Healthy Sexuality

We need to consider seriously the state of male sexuality
in these days of secularism and distorted family values and
design better ways for raising our children. Teaching teenagers
and younger children how to "protect" themselves isn't
enough. We need to teach them healthier attitudes, feelings,
and behaviors. We are never going to achieve a healthier society while male sexuality is out of control, as it seems to be in
these days—even among "good" Christian men.

The apostle Paul gave us the prescription in the New Testament when he wrote: "It is God's will that you should be
sanctified: that you should avoid sexual immorality; that each
of you should learn to control his own body in a way that is
holy and honorable, not in passionate lust like the heathen,
who do not know God" (1 Thess. 4:3–5).

The operative words here are, "Each of you should learn
to control his own body."

Merits of Self-Control

Every male making the transition from childhood through
adolescence to manhood has to develop a system of self-control over his sexuality. Why? First, because God requires it.
Second, because girls and women have a right to be protected

from a male's sex drive that is out of control. Third, because it helps the man to be a healthier, more fulfilled, godly person.

It alarms me how few parents of boys understand this. They believe that sexual control just happens. "Leave boys to themselves and it will all work out fine."

This isn't true at all. The sex drive is a powerful force, and like a high-spirited stallion, it needs to be brought under control if it is going to be the beautiful thing God intended it to be. So men, accept that it is your task with God's help to bring your sex drive under control. Accept that your sons must do the same, and model for them the healthiest sexuality you can.

What aspects of male sexuality need healing? Let's look at the most common areas:

Masturbation

One of the most vexing and complicated issues facing men today is the problem of masturbation. If men choose to remain celibate until marriage, many of them consider it the only sexual release available. Masturbation habits become deeply entrenched in most adolescent males.

Sixty-one percent of the married religious men in my study report that they continue to masturbate by themselves, mostly because they enjoy it. Wives complain bitterly about this. I have received several letters from wives and spoken to others on radio programs about husbands who lock themselves in the bathroom and masturbate. Many wives report that because of this habit, husbands often neglect sex in the marriage. Wives even feel punished by this neglect.

For a married man, masturbation by oneself has a negative effect on the relationship with his wife. It is especially a problem when he masturbates by himself, keeping it a secret from his wife. In doing so, he reclaims total authority over his body, which rightfully also belongs to his wife. "The husband's body does not belong to him alone but also to his wife" (1 Cor. 7:4). On the other hand, I believe that masturbation done together as a married couple is a normal, acceptable outlet for sexual fulfillment.

Masturbation has been a nagging issue for many single men. Some unmarried men waver on their opinion of masturbation for years, resulting in long-term guilt and confusion.

It is difficult for many men to masturbate without indulging in harmful lust and fantasy. Even so, some claim they use masturbation as a mechanical act without fantasy or pornography to release sexual pressure.

Because masturbation is habit-forming and it invites the sins of lust and fantasy, I cannot recommend it as a regular practice for single men. Those who avoid masturbation completely will reap the benefits: it's a powerful exercise in self-control, and it wards off temptation for destructive lust and fantasy.

Single men: I cannot quote to you a Bible verse that says, "Thou shalt not masturbate." But I can ask you to prayerfully consider the benefits of avoiding the practice and arrive at a course of action for your own life. It's time the single Christian men deal with this issue in a decisive manner and move on to other issues of great importance to God.

Pornography

So much has been written about pornography, including Len LeSourd's excellent article in the premier issue of *New Man*, that there is little I can add. My study shows that 71 percent of "good" men report that their exposure to pornography was destructive to their sexuality. Only 2 percent reported that it had some "educational" value. Yet 15.5 percent of married Christian men and nearly 7 percent of clergy continue to use pornography. It has become a sort of addiction for them.

Distortions to male sexuality, as my studies show, occur mainly during the early teens, and pornography is most boys' first sexual experience. Within a year or two after puberty, 98 percent of boys are exposed to pornography. Even if raised in a Christian home, 91 percent still report this exposure.

Few escape the influence of pornography. From it, boys learn to use sexual release for the wrong reasons. They become so accustomed to the "perfect" bodies of women in porn (mostly air-brushed with all flaws removed) that they rarely become satisfied with real and ordinary women.

Sexual Fantasies and Lust

More pervasive than pornography is how men use sexual fantasies to boost their sexual experiences. Twenty-five percent of the men in my study acknowledged that they "often" use fantasy during sex, while 45 percent reported that they "sometimes" use it.

What's wrong with fantasy? First, it is a violation against women; and second, fantasies later seek real fulfillment.

Lust is an obsession and unrelenting desire to have someone other than your wife as a sexual partner. It is a serious problem for many men. Good men agonize over the tensions this lust causes them, and a few succumb to it. In my sample of "good" married men, 59 percent fantasize about having sex with someone other than their wife.

There is a way to escape the chains of lust, fantasy, and other sexual pitfalls.

Steps for Change

What's the first step toward healing? It starts by admitting that something needs to change.

Take a long, honest look at your sexuality. Then, accept the forgiveness of God and stop flogging yourself for your sexual failures. Persistent guilt and shame will make it difficult to shed sexual problems.

Here are some steps I recommend for healthy sexuality:

1. Find someone you can trust and talk honestly about your sexual feelings.
2. Determine to change the way you think about women. When you look at a woman in sexual terms, catch

yourself and train your mind to view her in nonsexual ways.

3. Throw away all pornography.
4. Bring all your sexual thoughts and fantasies under conscious control by asking God to remind you when your thoughts need controlling.
5. Be honest about your feelings when you discuss your struggles with a trusted friend.
6. Acknowledge before God your lack of power to control your sexual urges, and pray that He will empower you to avoid temptation to sin by turning to healthy, wholesome activities.

In closing, let me remind you that sexual temptation is not sin. Some men are weakened by guilt from temptation. A pure mind is not a mind free of temptation. A pure mind chooses to act in the right way when temptation strikes.

My prayer for you is that you surrender your sexuality to God so that He can sanctify it and give it back to you in all its glory and purity.

A Conference You Must Attend

If you want to learn more about what makes a real man, plan a trip to a "Promise Keepers" conference. They're designed specifically to challenge men to true Christian manhood.

For more information, call (303) 421–2800 or write Promise Keepers, P.O. Box 18376, Boulder, CO 80308.

Resources to Get Your Hands On

- *What Makes a Man?* by Bill McCartney
- *A Man and His Loves* by Ray and Anne Ortlund
- *Promise Keepers* compiled by Focus on the Family
- *Brothers!* by Geoff Gorsuch
- *Hawk* by Andre Dawson
- *A Dad Who Loves You* by Bill Ritchie
- *The Man in the Mirror* by Patrick M. Morley
- *Maximized Manhood* by Edwin Louis Cole
- *Strategies for a Successful Marriage* by E. Glenn Wagner, Ph.D.
- *Victory* by A.C. Green

PART FIVE:

Horizons Filled With Hope

CHAPTER 16

A Compass That Comforts

It's pretty naive to think that God would speak to me through a tiny bit of Scripture printed on a two-dollar mug. But that's just what happened. Let me explain.

During a Saturday night banquet recently, my church welcomed a new youth pastor. It was supposed to be a first-rate celebration, complete with food, music, skits, and lots of laughs. But on that particular evening, I didn't feel like partying. I was in one of those moods, the kind only a single can relate to.

Not only was I having a bad hair day, Murphy's Law had hit hard: Everything that could possibly go wrong that day did. I was depressed, frazzled, weary, and at the end of my rope.

Susie was the emcee for the evening and asked everyone who worked with teens to come forward.

"We want our new youth guy to know just who you are!" she said. "And besides, you deserve a little pat on the back, too."

Come forward, I thought. Be recognized! I'd rather just sit here in the back of the hall and blend in—maybe even disappear.

The last place I wanted to be was at a church gathering, standing in the spotlight, even for a few brief minutes. But I mustered up my strength and grudgingly went forward.

After praying for the youth pastor and shaking his hand, we each received our introductions, along with a coffee mug filled with candy.

"You're looking at some true servants of God," said the pastor. "These folks are on the front lines, giving their time to your kids. This mug is just a token expression of how much we love you."

The church showered us with smiles and applause. It felt good to be appreciated, but I was still basking in a private, internal pity party.

As I headed back to my table, I glanced down at the newest addition to my mug collection.

Great, I thought, I got the one with the eagle. I love those birds.

Then I noticed a verse printed near the rim:

"But those who hope in the LORD will renew their strength. They will soar on wings like eagles; they will run and not grow weary, they will walk and not be faint" (Isaiah 41:31).

I froze in my tracks. I'd always tagged that passage as my "life verse." It was the one I pondered whenever my world turned upside down and my body felt like a feeble mass of nothingness.

Somehow I had forgotten about this verse. Thanks for the reminder, Lord.

As I sat down, my mind flashed back to the time in my life when that verse held special meaning.

A friend and I led a church group on a hike up a 12,000-foot mountain in Colorado—Pilot Peak, not far from Pikes Peak.

As we began our climb, the mountaintop stood before us like a compelling goal. All eyes were directed upward in awe. Our walk was brisk and the group cooperated unselfishly.

Less than two hours into the climb, the scene changed dramatically. The climb became arduous. Eyes were cast

downward and thoughts reflected inward. Our goal was forgotten. Tempers flared. Weariness set in and complaints stung
like thorns on the trail.

"Whose stupid idea was this?" one guy grumbled.

"We could be back at camp roasting marshmallows—anything but this!"

"Let's turn back . . . now!"

Right in the midst of near-anarchy I spotted a large bird
soaring above us . . . and that heaven-sent reminder popped
into my head: *"But those who hope in the Lord will renew
their strength. They will soar on wings like eagles."*

After some encouraging words and time spent in prayer,
my crew continued the climb and eventually reached the top!

Do you have a spiritual mountain to climb? Or is your
world more like a roller coaster . . . plunging into one problem
after another? Keep in mind that all Scripture is

- God-breathed
- sharper than a double-edged sword
- a compass that'll guide you through life's fiercest
  storms

So when times get tough, crack the Book. We've listed
some situations all singles face, along with Bible verses that
offer encouragement. Keep a bookmark in this chapter and
refer to it often. Better yet, write down some of these passages
on a three-by-five card and work on memorizing them.

When loneliness strikes . . .

If you love me, you will obey what I command. And I
will ask the Father, and he will give you another Coun-
selor to be with you forever—the Spirit of truth. The
world cannot accept him, because it neither sees him
nor knows him. But you know him, for he lives with
you and will be in you. I will not leave you as orphans;
I will come to you (John 14:15–18).

When you're gripped with fear . . .

The Lord is my light and my salvation—whom shall I fear? The Lord is the stronghold of my life—of whom shall I be afraid? (Psalm 27:1).

So do not fear, for I am with you; do not be dismayed, for I am your God. I will strengthen you and help you; I will uphold you with my righteous right hand (Isaiah 41:10).

When doubt creeps in . . .

I am the way and the truth and the life. No one comes to the Father except through me. If you really knew me, you would know my Father as well. From now on, you do know him and have seen him (John 14:6–7).

I have come into the world as a light, so that no one who believes in me should stay in darkness. As for the person who hears my words but does not keep them, I do not judge him. For I did not come to judge the world, but to save it (John 12:46–47).

When you look in the mirror and hate what you see . . .

For you created my inmost being; you knit me together in my mother's womb. I praise you because I am fearfully and wonderfully made; your works are wonderful, I know that full well. My frame was not hidden from you when I was made in the secret place. When I was woven together in the depths of the earth, your eyes saw my unformed body. All the days ordained for me were written in your book before one of them came to be (Psalm 139:13–16).

I tell you the truth, anyone who has faith in me will do what I have been doing. He will do even greater things than these, because I am going to the Father. And I will do whatever you ask in my name, so that the Son may bring glory to the Father. You may ask me for anything in my name, and I will do it (John 14:12–14).

When you're fed up with being single . . .

I wish that all men were as I am. But each man has his own gift from God; one has this gift, another has that. Now to the unmarried and the widows I say: It is good for them to stay unmarried, as I am (1 Corinthians 7:7–8).

For this very reason, make every effort to add to your faith goodness; and to goodness, knowledge; and to knowledge, self-control; and to self-control, perseverance; and to perseverance, godliness; and to godliness, brotherly kindness; and to brotherly kindness, love. For if you possess these qualities in increasing measure, they will keep you from being ineffective and unproductive in your knowledge of our Lord Jesus Christ (2 Peter 1:5–8).

When hope vanishes . . .

For the eyes of the LORD range throughout the earth to strengthen those whose hearts are fully committed to him (2 Chronicles 16:9).

I waited patiently for the LORD; he turned to me and heard my cry. He lifted me out of the slimy pit, out of the mud and mire; he set my feet on a rock and gave me a firm place to stand (Psalm 40:1–2).

The LORD is righteous in all his ways and loving toward all he has made. The LORD is near to all who call on him, to all who call on him in truth. He fulfills the desires of those who fear him; he hears their cry and saves them (Psalm 145:17–19).

There is surely a future hope for you, and your hope will not be cut off (Proverbs 23:18).

Come to me, all you who are weary and burdened, and I will give you rest. Take my yoke upon you and learn from me, for I am gentle and humble in heart, and you will find rest for your souls. For my yoke is easy and my burden is light (Matthew 11:28–30).

But hope that is seen is no hope at all. Who hopes for what he already has? But if we hope for what we do not yet have, we wait for it patiently. In the same way, the Spirit helps us in our weakness. We do not know what we ought to pray, but the Spirit himself intercedes for us with groans that words cannot express (Romans 8:24–26).

Remember, when you're lonely, depressed, or caught in the trap of self-pity, God's Word is the only comfort that really lasts. It is the only stable anchor in this world of temporary harbors.

CHAPTER 17

In the Arms of Love Without Getting Strangled

Tiffany leans back and rests her head on my shoulder. I munch a handful of popcorn, then wrap my arms around her. Neither one of us takes our eyes off the TV. We are glued to our all-time favorite comedy flick—*The Princess Bride.*

"Oo, oo! I love this part," I blurt, reaching for some more popcorn.

Tiffany jabs my side. "You said that three scenes ago. Now stop talking!"

On the screen before us, the hotshot swordsman—Inigo Montoya—and his enormous sidekick, Andre the Giant, just rescued Wesley from the king's torture rack. Their mission: reunite the stable boy with his true love—Princess Buttercup. But there is one problem. Wesley is mostly dead.

That's when the motley crew visits Miracle Max (Billy Crystal) for a cure.

"Oh, my mistake! Now *this* is my favorite part, Tiff. Not that last scene—"

"Quiet!"

"He-e-e-y! Hello in there," Max says as he looks down Wesley's throat. "What's so important? Whatcha got here that's worth living for?"

The "miracle man" presses Wesley's stomach, forcing a breath of air from the young man's lips . . . along with the words, "Tr-u-u-ue love."

Inigo's eyes light up. "True love! Did you hear him? You could not ask for a more noble cause than that."

Max agrees. "True love *is* the greatest thing in the world."

Tiffany glances up at me and grins.

I gently hug her and kiss her cheek. (This is beginning to sound as sappy as the dialogue in *The Princess Bride,* but this is one of the best parts of dating.)

"I love these moments," Tiffany says.

"It's a little bit of heaven, isn't it?"

I can't imagine anyone else I'd rather be with, I tell myself. *I can't imagine spending a day without this woman. Have I found my one true love?*

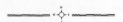

Nearly all singles share the dream of finding the love of their life. For some, the search is easy. But for others, the path to matrimonial bliss is brutally bumpy, causing them to wonder if the adventure is even worth it.

"I'm not on a desperate search for a mate," says one single. "I know 'the grass isn't greener' on the other side. Just ask my married friends."

Counter that with this quote from a married man: "Next to my faith in Jesus, my marriage is the most precious thing in my life."

As I write this chapter, I must be brutally honest with you: My own dating adventure has been full of potholes and has often left me feeling rather anxious about this whole romance thing. But my current relationship with Tiffany has been the breath of fresh air I need. It has brought about a lot of deep healing and growth in my life.

Marriage could be a short hike down the trail for me. Tiffany could very well be the life mate who's an ideal fit. But then again, God may have other plans for the two of us. And that's okay, too.

Throughout this book Susie and I have talked honestly about our need to love and to be loved and how the foundation of love must come from our relationship with Jesus. That's the key to filling the void.

But here's the question of the hour: Once you've fallen head over heels for someone, how do you know for sure what you've found is in fact true love—the kind that'll last a lifetime? What's more, why do so many married couples start out on smooth waters only to find themselves facing a tidal wave? And what can a single do before marriage to prevent disaster later?

Poll twenty people and you'll probably end up with twenty different answers to these questions. Each relationship is different. But I've discovered some basic keys along the way that I'm confident will help me open the treasure of true love, prepare me for my future wife . . . and set us sailing on a smooth course.

We'll use my relationship with Tiffany as a case study (she said it would be okay). So let's head back to my house and the movie we were watching . . . and listen in on our conversation afterward. It reveals a lot about the health of our relationship.

THE SEARCH FOR TRUE LOVE

As the movie credits fill the screen and I punch rewind on the remote, Tiffany looks me in the eyes.

"The movie's over and now you stop talking," she says with a grin. "I can see those wheels spinning inside. What's on your mind?"

I smile. "You."

"And . . ."

"And how awesome God is for making such an incredible person—you—then giving you to me. And I was thinking how awesome God is for giving us wonderful gifts like closeness and love."

Tiffany turns to face me. "Wow," she says, grinning. "That's a change from the guys I've dated in the past. Most of them wouldn't have had God on their minds while they were on a date. They seemed to be motivated by their hormones."

"Well, those guys were obviously selfish boys," I tell her. "I respect you, Tiff. I could never imagine using you . . . that would break my heart."

"Now that's a first," she says, then gives me another kiss. "And it's a first I like."

Our relationship is filled with a lot of firsts . . . a number of elements that make for a solid relationship.

With Tiffany . . .

- I can relax and be myself
- I don't have to fear that she'll think badly about something I say or do
- I never have to wear a mask when I'm around her
- I never feel I'm in competition with her
- I feel supported
- I feel challenged
- I never detect jealousy from her
- I trust her completely
- I make sacrifices to be with her
- I miss her when we're apart

So far, we're both experiencing green lights in our relationship. But somewhere deep inside, we're aware of a little voice that warns: "Bravo, Tiffany . . . bravo, Michael. You two are in the 'Disneyland' phase of your relationship. But can you hold up under the storms that are just over the horizon?"

Working at a place like Focus on the Family has made me aware of a disturbing fact: Marriages are under attack as never before. It's hard to find a truly happy married couple. Experts estimate that more than twenty million American couples live in desperate unhappiness.

But I don't believe it has to be that way. I once read that "marriage can be the closest thing to heaven on earth if we do it God's way. Or it can be the closest thing to hell on earth. . . . The choice is ours."

The key points to ponder are "God's way" and "choice." Marriage can be something strong and wonderful if we take God's standards seriously and commit our hearts to him.

With this in mind, here's a strategy we've chosen to follow:

We're Committed to Purity

Why didn't God make it easy? Why not give us sexual desires on our wedding day and not before? I don't know why. But I do know I wouldn't like to be without sexual desires. I like being human, hard as it is. I'm thankful God trusted me with the challenge.

Author Tim Stafford made the preceding comments in his book *Love, Sex and the Whole Person.* And I couldn't agree more. Waiting is hard, but I'm thankful God designed us just as he did. And Tiffany and I both believe that waiting is worth it.

We believe that sex before marriage—sex without complete commitment—is like dessert before the meal. It could spoil our appetite for really healthy food. People who have sex without commitment usually never get to the commitment. People who try sex without marriage find it hard to create lasting, loving relationships.

Unlike any other experience between a married couple, sexual intercourse creates the deepest, most powerful bond . . .

sort of a relational Super Glue. And that bond is never supposed to be separated. Sex isn't just something physical that feels good for a few seconds. Sex involves a couple's bodies, minds, and emotions in an activity that is intended to continue for a lifetime.

"Why would anyone want to mess up something beautiful God has created?" Tiffany once asked me. "It just makes sense to wait."

We both are committed to this.

We're Preparing Now for Marriage

As Susie and I have said in earlier chapters, right now as a single person, you can prepare yourself to be the husband or wife your future mate needs.

And that's exactly what Tiffany and I are seeking to do. If the Lord so leads, perhaps marriage will come from this relationship. But whether it does or not, our days of courtship are not insignificant. We are establishing habits right now that will carry through into our future marriages. We're establishing certain ways of communicating that will continue for years to come.

I like what Pastor Greg Laurie has to say on this matter. In his book *God's Design for Christian Dating,* he writes:

> Now is the time to lay a spiritual foundation. Now is the time to establish good habits with your mate, such as praying together, studying the Bible together, participating in fellowship with other Christians at church, and even witnessing together.
>
> As you lay these foundations and build upon them in years to come, your relationship will stand strong. Every marriage will have its storms. Every marriage will have its difficulties.

We're Entrusting This Relationship to God

The outcome is in his hands. That's the bottom line. And that involves prayer and listening to him.

But I must admit that being patient isn't easy. Sometimes my prayers go something like this: *Lord, you know how I feel about Tiffany. Please give us the green light . . . please let us be married. Before I get up off my knees, let me know if I should pop the question today.*

Then I pause quietly and a cool truth enters my mind: "Don't seek your will . . . but God's. Trust him in this and all circumstances. His way is the right way."

I have come to realize that it may take a period of patient waiting before God speaks to us about an issue—especially something as important as marriage. Why? Because he has forgotten or because our question is not that important to him? Absolutely not! In the process of waiting he is preparing us for his answer, which we may have missed had he spoken immediately.

According to author Charles Stanley in his book *How to Listen to God,*

> The Lord will not tell us some things instantaneously. We will hear some special revelations only after having waited a season of time. We're not always ready, so God will sometimes withhold information until we are prepared to listen.
>
> We must be willing to listen to Him patiently because these times may draw out and stretch our faith. He has promised to speak to our hearts, so we can expect Him to, but He is not compelled to tell us everything we want to know the moment we desire the information.

We'll Never Settle for an Imitation

In the words of Miracle Max, "True love is the greatest thing in the world." It's priceless—more precious than the finest rubies.

And that's exactly how Max Lucado describes it. He has a way of telling a story like no one else, and my favorite is a delightful tale called "The Secret of Love." It is told through the eyes of Asmara, a merchant of fine stones. He grew up long ago in Morocco and learned a hard lesson about true love. He discovered—too late—that it's not unlike finding an authentic jewel.

Let me share this story with you. And as we end our journey together, keep in mind Max's wise advice. It just might save your heart from major attack.

These words are ancient jewels mined from the quarry of life. Read them only if you dare treasure them. For it would be better to never know than to know and not obey.

The hand that writes them is now old, wrinkled from the sun and labor. But the mind that guides them is wise—wise from years, wise from failures, wise from heartache.

I travel from city to city. I buy jewels from the diggers in one land and sell them to the buyers in another. I have weathered nights on stormy waters. I have walked days through desert heat. My hands have held the finest rubies and stroked the deepest furs. But I would trade it all for the one jewel I never knew.

It was not for lack of opportunity that I never held it. It was for lack of wisdom. The jewel was in my hand, but I exchanged it for an imitation.

I have never known true love.

I have known embraces. I have seen beauty. But I have never known love.

If only I'd learned to recognize love as I have learned to recognize stones.

My father taught me about stones. He was a jewel cutter. He would seat me at a table before a dozen emeralds.

"One is true," he would tell me. "The others are false. Find the true jewel."

I would ponder—studying one after the other. Finally I would choose. I was always wrong.

"The secret," he would say, "is not on the surface of the stone; it is inside the stone. A true jewel has a glow. Deep within the gem there is a flame. The surface can always be polished to shine, but with time the sparkle fades. However, the stone that shines from within will never fade."

With years, my eyes learned to spot true stones. I am never fooled. I have learned to see the light within.

If only I'd learned the same about love.

But I've spent my life in places I shouldn't have been, looking only for someone with beautiful hair, a dazzling smile and fancy clothes. I've searched for a woman with outer beauty but no true value. And now I am left with *emptiness.*

Once I almost found her. Many years ago in Madrid I met the daughter of a farmer. Her ways were simple. Her love was pure. Her eyes were honest. But her looks were plain. She would have loved me. She would have held me through every season. Within her was a glow of devotion the likes of which I've never seen since.

But I continued looking for someone whose beauty would outshine the rest.

How many times since have I longed for that farm girl's kind heart? If only I'd known that true beauty is found inside, not outside. If only I'd known, how many tears would I have saved?

True love glows from within and grows stronger with the passage of time.

Heed my caution. Look for the purest gem. Look deep within the heart to find the greatest beauty of all. And when you find that gem, hold onto her and never let her go.

For in her you have been granted a treasure worth far more than rubies.

Seek beauty and miss love.

But seek love and find both.

———— ◇ ————

Have I found a jewel in my relationship with Tiffany? Most definitely. Have I found true love . . . a soul mate to spend my life with? Only time will tell.

Jewels to Ponder

Authentic Love

- Psalm 36:5–12
- Matthew 5:43–48
- Acts 3:1–10
- 1 Corinthians 13:1–13
- 1 John 4:7–14
- 1 John 4:15–21

How to Find Treasure

- Psalm 51
- Proverbs 4:1–13
- Proverbs 4:14–27
- Galatians 5:16–26
- Ephesians 5:1–21
- 1 Thessalonians 4:6–12

Ultimate Love

- John 15:9–15
- Jeremiah 31:3
- Romans 5:1–11
- Romans 8:31–39
- Ephesians 3:16–21
- 1 John 3:11–24

CHAPTER 18

One Last Thing About Love

We've mentioned it numerous times already, but the key to escaping the Poor Me Syndrome that so many singles fall into is to invest yourself in the lives of those around you.

One of my (Susie's) favorite children's books is *If You Give a Mouse a Cookie* by Laura Joffe Numeroff. It's an exaggerated tale of what might happen if one actually did give a mouse a cookie. The author tells us if we give the rodent a cookie, he'll want some milk to go with it. And then he'll have to look in a mirror to make sure he doesn't have a milk mustache. Then he'll notice his hair needs a trim, so he'll probably ask for a pair of scissors. The story goes on and on and on in creative detail of the demands a mouse could make.

After I read the book for the first time, I closed it with a smile thinking, *Enough said. The moral of the story is "Never give a mouse a cookie!"*

But the more I thought about it, I sensed the Lord was trying to teach me something. (Yes, sometimes he has to resort to children's books to catch my attention.) God could have adapted the same moral. He didn't give his children a cookie. Yet, he gave the greatest gift in all the world—his only Son.

If our heavenly Father could give his own flesh and blood, how much more should we be willing to give our lives to those around us!

It's not easy, though. After all, when we give a mouse a cookie, he will ask for a glass of milk . . . and a million other things.

When we invest our time and ourselves in people, we can assume they're going to ask for more. If I invite my neighbor to church, I'll probably have to let her ride with me. Then I'll have to sit with her because she won't know anyone.

Then after Sunday school, I'll have to walk her into the sanctuary. And after church is over, I'll probably have to take her to dinner. And if she enjoys our church, I'll have to bring her again. And again. And again.

And if she gives her life to the Lord, I might have to disciple her. Or go to Bible study with her. So I just better stay away completely.

That's pretty silly, isn't it?

God asks us to give our time, our energy, and ourselves to those around us because that's exactly what he does. He could have said, "I'd better not leave heaven and invade their world with love. If I do, they'll probably ask me to help them. Then I'll have to do a few miracles. Heal some people. Pass out some 20/20 to a few blind men. And those who don't like me will probably kill me. Then I'll have to raise myself from the dead and send my Spirit to live within them. And I'll have to prepare a home for them to live in eternally. It'll never end!"

Whew!

I'm glad our Father didn't take that kind of attitude. Instead, he chooses to invade our lives with purpose, meaning, drive, and power. In return, he calls us to give away some cookies. To spread a little love. To be him to a lost and dying world.

And if we do? We forget about our singleness. Suddenly, it's just not important anymore. Rather, meeting the needs of others becomes a significant priority.

SHE WENT THE EXTRA MILE

My office usually looks like the birthplace of Hurricane Hilda. Papers, magazines, books, boxes, tapes, CDs . . . you name it and it's sitting in my office.

One particular time my office became ridiculously hideous. When things actually came to life and crawled into the offices surrounding mine, my co-workers began to nag me.

My friend Cheryl was in town—but on vacation. She heard about the mess and marched into the hurricane with a fierce determination to organize the storm. It was incredible. She moved in a whirlwind of logic and purpose. She stacked letters, tossed old papers, and obtained a brand-new stack of file folders. She proceeded to create labels for each folder, then turned to me and said, "Susie, why don't we make a file for everything on your desk?"

Okay, maybe this is hard to believe . . . but I'd never thought of that before. "File it?" I said. "What a novel idea!" In four hours she had my office looking like the executive suite.

I ran home, grabbed my Crock-Pot and those little beanie-wienies, poured in some barbecue sauce, took it back to the office, and plugged it in. Lisa ran to the grocery store and bought a cheese ball. Susan found some crackers, Chuck grabbed some paper plates, and we threw a party in my "new" office.

Because organization comes naturally for Cheryl, cleaning and rearranging my office seemed like second nature to her. To me . . . she had just given me a giant cookie. She had walked the extra mile. I'll never forget it!

Last year I traveled to Uganda, Africa, to do a story for *Brio* magazine on kids orphaned because of AIDS. I bought several bags of candy before I left the States, and when I visited the schools, I passed out treats to the children.

At one particular school, the principal had them all line up in single rows to receive their candy. He grabbed a few sixth-grade boys and said, "Let them help you pass out the candy so it won't take as long."

I reluctantly handed over half of the treats and cringed inside because I was afraid they'd keep most of the candy for themselves.

But I watched them. When we ran low on stock, they began to break the pieces in half. When a piece dropped on the ground, I was amazed as a child would bend over, pick it up, and give it to someone who hadn't received any yet. They were so willing to share. And when we were at the bottom of our supply, my sixth-grade helpers quickly gave their own piece of candy to others who hadn't received any.

They were going the extra mile. They were so concerned that the younger children get a piece of candy they didn't even think of their own desires.

That's exactly what makes our heavenly Father smile. As singles, though, it's easy to fall into a selfish mindset. We often adopt a "me" philosophy. "I better watch out for myself because no one else is." Or "I need to make sure I'm not taken advantage of just because I'm single. So I'll shout louder, make my demands, and aggressively move forward."

How can we be giving cookies away if we're so concerned about our own refreshments? Again God calls us to go the extra mile. Why?

- Because he did
- Because in order to find ourselves, we must give away our lives
- Because giving, loving, and going the extra mile causes us to forget about our aloneness
- Because we grow by sacrificing
- Because love always wins

IT'S A THING CALLED LOVE

So how about it? Instead of focusing on *your* needs, *your* desires, *your* problems, will you choose, instead, to throw yourself into those around you? And while you're at it . . . remind yourself what God has to say about cookie-giving. He calls it genuine love. Go ahead. Take a fresh new look at the love chapter: 1 Corinthians 13 from *The Message* (The New Testament in Contemporary English).

If I speak with human eloquence and angelic ecstasy but don't love, I'm nothing but the creaking of a rusty gate.

If I speak God's Word with power, revealing all his mysteries and making everything plain as day, and if I have faith that says to a mountain, "Jump," and it jumps, but I don't love, I'm nothing.

If I give everything I own to the poor and even go to the stake to be burned as a martyr, but I don't love, I've gotten nowhere. So, no matter what I say, what I believe, and what I do, I'm bankrupt without love.

Love never gives up.
Love cares more for others than for self.
Love doesn't want what it doesn't have.
Love doesn't strut,
Doesn't have a swelled head,
Doesn't force itself on others,
Isn't always "me first,"
Doesn't fly off the handle,
Doesn't keep score of the sins of others,
Doesn't revel when others grovel,
Takes pleasure in the flowering of truth,
Puts up with anything,
Trusts God always,

Always looks for the best,
Never looks back,
But keeps going to the end.

Love never dies. Inspired speech will be over some day; praying in tongues will end; understanding will reach its limit. We know only a portion of the truth, and what we say about God is always incomplete. But when the Complete arrives, our incompletes will be canceled.

When I was an infant at my mother's breast, I gurgled and cooed like any infant. When I grew up, I left those infant ways for good.

We don't yet see things clearly. We're squinting in a fog, peering through a mist. But it won't be long before the water clears and the sun shines bright! We'll see it all then, see it all as clearly as God sees us, knowing him directly just as he knows us!

But for right now, until that completeness, we have three things to do to lead us toward that consummation: trust steadily in God, hope unswervingly, love extravagantly. And the best of the three is love.